REVELATION IN THE VERNACULAR

DISRUPTIVE CARTOGRAPHERS:
DOING THEOLOGY LATINAMENTE

Series editors: Carmen M. Nanko-Fernández,
Miguel H. Díaz, Gary Riebe-Estrella

This multivolume series re-maps theology and pushes out in new directions from varying coordinates across a spectrum of latinidad as lived in the USA. Authors reconfigure and disrupt key areas like revelation, pneumatology, eschatology, and Mariology. Other volumes complicate and advance even further key themes of significance in Latin@ theologies, including the option for culture, religious diversity, and the integral relationship between theologizing and praxis.

Previously published:

Miguel H. Díaz, editor, *The Word Became Culture*

Disruptive Cartographers: Doing Theology Latinamente

REVELATION IN THE VERNACULAR

JEAN-PIERRE RUIZ

Fordham University Press
New York   2024

Every scribe who has been trained for the kingdom of

heaven is like the master of a household who brings

out of his treasure what is new and what is old.

—Matthew 13:52 *NRSV*

In grateful remembrance of Raymond E. Brown, S.S.,

Ugo Vanni, S.J., David A. Sánchez, and Robert M.

Robinson, scribes trained for the kingdom of heaven.

CONTENTS

Preface to the Series

Disruptive Cartographers

Maps are functional and aesthetic. They establish and make visible place, space, time, and distance in terms of scale and relationships that are inevitably influenced by the cartographer's own coordinates. Mapping as a process is not as objective as it might seem, and the maps produced are not beyond bias. Maps are tools of power employed by empires to mark and represent their domains, territorially, economically, politically, culturally, religiously. Mapping also orients resistance by contesting borders, shifting perspective, challenging omissions, retrieving what was rendered invisible or insignificant, disrupting the illusion that certain maps or particular ways of mapping are necessarily normative.

Disruptive Cartographers is a multivolume series mapping theology from varying coordinates across a spectrum of latinidad as lived in the USA. Points of departure for Latin@ theologies are embedded in the complexities of la vida cotidiana, daily lived experience, which call forth a rich variety of responses from theologians who self-identify, in roots and commitments, as belonging to and emerging from the diversity found under such umbrella terms as Hispanic, Latino/a, Latinx, Latin@, Latin@. Explorations of lo cotidiano require a variety of lenses that must take into account intricate historical constructions that cannot easily shake off legacies of racism, sexism, heterosexism, classism, ableism, and colonialism. These legacies and their contemporary manifestations continue to influence sociopolitical contexts, theological formulations, and power and privilege differentials in church, academy, and society. The authors in this series have been left free to choose their own lenses and to probe those historical trajectories which most reflect their experience of the subject at hand.

In this series in constructive theology some volumes seek to reconfigure such key areas as revelation, pneumatology, and eschatology, and others pursue themes significant in theologizing latinamente, including the option for culture, religious pluralism, and the relationship between theory and praxis. Each volume retrieves sources from within the historical stream of Latin@ theologies using contemporary experience as a guide. This series is not an introduction to Latino/a theology; it is not a comprehensive survey of contemporary Latinx theology; it is not an attempt to assert a monolithic or foundational Latin@ theology. Each volume offers a distinctive perspective on a topic familiar to systematic theologians. Accomplished latinamente, each reveals the complexity, diversity, and theological creativity that continues to emerge from within the community of Latino, Latina, Latinx theologians and scholars.

This distinctiveness is evident across the series volumes in a variety of ways. Within Latin@ theologies, socially locating one's perspective is an ethical obligation, an admission that our complicated identities and situated places from which we theologize form, inform, and reform our scholarship. Our fluid identities are expressed through a multiplicity of terms by which we name ourselves (Latino/a, Latinao, Latinoa, Latin@, Latin@, Latinx, Hispanic, Hispana, Hispano, Chican@, Tejana, Boricua, Cuban American are but a few). This self-naming is not a matter of semantics or political correctness but a claim that identity is a matter of theological anthropology. In this series there is no one imposed term, and each author provides their own rationale for their preferences. In addition, Latin@ theologies operate at the intersection of languages, and this hybridity may be reflected in the deployment of English, Spanish, and variations of Spanglish within texts. For Latinos/as Spanish is not a foreign language, and authors may choose not to italicize it in their respective volumes. Our preference for footnotes over endnotes reflects an understanding that they engage in a conversation literally on the same page as the body text. In this (at times) multilingual *conjunto* each maintains its integrity, and it is easier for readers to move from one to the other smoothly.

While each volume offers a distinctive and not a comprehensive perspective, authors situate themselves within the larger enterprise of doing theology latinamente and demonstrate that commitment by underscoring the relevance of lived experience as locus theologicus and by retrieving resources that draw from the depth and breadth of latinidad. Readers can begin their reading with any of the volumes in this series. Their commonality is to be found in the methods authors use to theologize; their diversity is in the historical sources and daily experience they privilege.

Ultimately, this series acknowledges that theological mapping matters for our communities of accountability too long left off or consigned to the margins of too many maps. At the same time, by allowing for creative and sustained development of constructive theological threads, familiar yet new, this series seeks to emulate the advice of Pope Francis to theologians: "Do not lose the ability for wonder; to practice theology in wonder."[1]

Carmen M. Nanko-Fernández,
Gary Riebe-Estrella, Miguel H. Díaz
Series Editors

---

[1] Pope Francis, "Audience with Members of the Italian Theological Association," December 29, 2017, http://press.vatican.va/content/sala-stampa/en/bollettino/pubblico/2017/12/29/171229c.html.

Acknowledgments

As editors of the series in which this book appears, Disruptive Cartographers: Doing Theology Latinamente, editors Carmen Nanko-Fernández, Gary Riebe-Estrella, and Miguel H. Díaz dare to think differently, taking the risk of encouraging authors to remap and reconfigure key sites on the theological landscape, to contest conventional normative claims and to bring to light new sources and new approaches. The authors in this series have been invited, borrowing a phrase from Pope Francis, "¡Hagan lío!" In this volume about revelation in the vernacular, it makes sense to point out that the usual English translation, "make a mess," falls short, and "shake things up" captures the sense of the phrase far better. I am grateful for the invitation the series editors extended to me to shake things up a bit in these pages about revelation, and I hope the mess I have deliberately made in these pages invites readers to remap revelation in ways they might not have considered before.

Ecclesiastes 12:12 warns, "Of making many books there is no end, and much study is a weariness of the flesh," yet—with due respect but without deference to the biblical author of that verse— books can stir mind and heart and spirit even if they can weary the flesh. For that reason, I offer heartfelt thanks to those in the world of publishing who made this book possible, who welcomed the project at various stages and saw it through to publication. Among them are Michael Gibson, Robert Ellsberg, Maria Angelini, and John Garza with his colleagues at Fordham University Press. I especially appreciate the balance between great patience and gentle persistence with which they nudged this project to its completion, even amidst the formidable challenges of the Covid-19 pandemic.

It is my privilege to serve as a member of the faculty of the Department of Theology and Religious Studies at St. John's University in New York. For a century and a half, St. John's has worked to reshape the landscape of higher education in ways that empower marginalized and minoritized communities. I deeply appreciate the ways in which the university's commitment to its mission has provided energy for my work in the classroom and at the writing desk, and I am especially grateful for the many ways in which my department colleagues Jeremy V. Cruz and Robert J. "Bobby" Rivera make *teología de conjunto* so real for me.

While I have already expressed my thanks to Carmen Nanko-Fernández in her capacity as one of the co-conspirers who thought this series into existence and whose inspiration so effectively energizes the work of the series authors, I would be seriously negligent if I did not also acknowledge with gratitude the debt I owe to her own example as a disruptive cartographer. It takes genuine courage to think differently and to write in ways that challenge conventional thinking in the service of justice, and Carmen does so with the kind of eloquence than only a fellow New Yorker can fully appreciate. I hope that the Nuyorican voice that speaks in these pages measures up to the integrity that Carmen models so very well.

The Latin@ practice of *teología de conjunto* recognizes that the work of theology thrives in the first-person plural, and so I give thanks to God for, and express my deep gratitude to those who have inspired this project and who have contributed to it whether directly or indirectly, among them Orlando O. Espín, Jonathan Y. Tan, C. Vanessa White, Edwin Aponte, Laura Jakubowski Aponte, Jacqueline Hidalgo, Elieser Valentín, Efraín Agosto, Connie Fernández, David Maldonado-Rivera, and Krag Kerr, together with the staff of the Paul Bechtold Library of the Catholic Theological Union in Chicago, especially Kris Veldheer and Aileen Mulchrone. While I owe much to them and to many others for any merits this book may have, its shortcomings are mine alone. Finally, I offer special thanks to Darién Farel Irizarry, whose original artwork, "Sol Revelado," created with this book in mind, is the painting that graces the cover. It so magnificently expresses what the words of this book struggle mightily to communicate.

INTRODUCTION

Revelation a Long Way from Patmos

When friends and colleagues learned that I was working on a book on the theology of revelation, many of them assumed almost automatically that I was writing about the last book of the New Testament canon, the Apocalypse, the Revelation to John. Theirs was a fair enough assumption, because I have devoted considerable attention to the interpretation of the book of Revelation.[1]

---

[1] See, for example, Jean-Pierre Ruiz, *Ezekiel in the Apocalypse: The Transformation of Prophetic Language in Revelation 16,17–19,10* (European University Studies; Frankfurt am Main: Peter Lang, 1989); idem, "Taking a Stand on the Sand of the Seashore: A Postcolonial Exploration of Revelation 13," in *Reading the Book of Revelation: A Resource for Students,* ed. David L. Barr (Atlanta, GA: Scholars Press, 2003), 119–136; idem, "Hearing and Seeing but Not Saying: A Rhetoric of Authority in Revelation 10:2 and 2 Corinthians 12:4," in *The Reality of Apocalypse: Rhetoric and Politics in the Book of Revelation,* ed. David L. Barr (Atlanta, GA: Society of Biblical Literature, 2006), 91–111; idem, "The Bible and the Exegesis of Empire: Reading Christopher Columbus's *El libro de las profecías,*" in Jean-Pierre Ruiz, *Readings from the Edges: The Bible & People on the Move* (Maryknoll, NY: Orbis Books, 2011), 123–139; idem, "The Mighty City and the Holy City: John's Apocalypse at the Intersections of Power and Praise," *The Living Pulpit,* August 17, 2015, http://www.pulpit.org/the-mighty-city-and-the-holy-city-johns-apocalypse-at-the-intersections-of-power-and-praise/. Also see Jean-Pierre Ruiz, "The Revelation to John," in *The New Oxford Annotated Bible: New Revised Standard Version with the Apocrypha,* ed. Michael D. Coogan, Marc Z. Brettler, Carol A. Newsom, and Pheme Perkins (Fifth Edition; New York: Oxford University Press, 2018), 2203–2205.

The trajectory of my work on the Revelation to John has become more and more explicitly and deliberately a matter of biblical interpretation done *latinamente*, an approach I have characterized as collaborative, connected, and committed.[2] While I admit that the long shadow (or is it light?) cast by the Apocalypse and my work on that rich and perplexing text has influenced the thinking that informs this book, this project takes up a challenge to which I made reference in an earlier publication, where I identified a significant and persistent lacuna. As I observed, "Surprisingly enough, while passing mention has been made here and there in U.S. Latino/a Christian theology of what we assume we mean when we speak of revelation, there has been very little sustained exploration of this foundational notion."[3] As I also noted, in the pages of the very first issue of the *Journal of Hispanic / Latino Theology*, published in 1993, Sixto J. Garcia wrote:

> We hold, as a foundational belief, that the Scriptures are the Word of God. To even attempt to engage ourselves in a discussion concerning the interpretation of this statement would be to open a can of hermeneutical worms quite peripheral to our discussion. It is legitimate to say, however, that regardless of the different theological contours that different people might draw concerning "Scriptures as Word of God," we hold in common the normative dimension of the Scriptures (the Scriptures

---

[2] See Jean-Pierre Ruiz, "The Bible and Latino/a Theology," in *The Wiley Blackwell Companion to Latino/a Theology*, ed. Orlando O. Espín (Malden, MA: Wiley Blackwell, 2015), 111–127.

[3] Jean-Pierre Ruiz, "The Word became Flesh and the Flesh Becomes Word: Notes Toward a U.S. Latino/a Theology of Revelation," in *Building Bridges, Doing Justice: Constructing a Latino/a Ecumenical Theology*, ed. Orlando O. Espín (Maryknoll, NY: Orbis Books, 2009), 51.

are the soul of all theology) for theological reflection on God's self-communication.[4]

In my earlier essay, I very modestly took it upon myself to begin to open the can of hermeneutical worms about which García sagely warned. The limited scope of that essay allowed me only to sketch some very preliminary notes toward a U.S. Latin@ theology of revelation.[5] This book represents an effort to take another step or two in that direction. I do so while gratefully aware that the lacuna in Latin@ theology to which I drew attention has been addressed very capably both in an essay by biblical scholar Efraín Agosto that was published in *The Wiley Blackwell Companion to Latino/a Theology* and in *Dogmatics after Babel*, an important book by theologian Rubén Rosario Rodríguez, both fellow Puerto Ricans.[6]

Agosto begins with definitions, starting with Rosemary Carbine's succinct "divine self-disclosure," then Jaroslav Pelikan's

---

[4] Ruiz, "The Word Became Flesh and the Flesh Becomes Word," 51, citing Sixto J. García, "Sources and Loci of Hispanic Theology," *Journal of Hispanic / Latino Theology* 1, no. 1 (November 1993): 22–43; reprinted in *Mestizo Christianity: Theology from the Latino Perspective*, ed. Arturo J. Bañuelas (Maryknoll, NY: Orbis Books, 1995), 108.

[5] I use "Latin@" throughout this book, while remaining acutely conscious of the enormous challenges that are involved in considering the many diverse communities and individuals "whose cultural and historical roots are to be found in Latin America" (Orlando O. Espín, "Introduction," in *The Wiley Blackwell Companion to Latino/a Theology*, 1, and see Espín's helpful overview of the expression "Latinos/as" on pages 1–3). Also see Carmen Nanko-Fernández, *Theologizing en Espanglish: Context, Community, and Ministry* (Maryknoll, NY: Orbis Books, 2010), xv–xvi.

[6] Efraín Agosto, "Revelation," in *The Wiley Blackwell Companion to Latino/a Theology*, ed. Orlando O. Espín (Malden, MA: Wiley Blackwell, 2015), 91–109; Rubén Rosario Rodríguez, *Dogmatics after Babel: Beyond the Theologies of Word and Culture* (Louisville, KY: Westminster John Knox, 2018).

description of revelation as "the self-disclosure of God and the communication of the truth about [God's] nature and will," and then Gerhard Sauter's invocation of *apokalypsis* in his description of revelation as a matter of "unveiling what was hidden."[7] Agosto then goes on to survey the landscape of Latin@ Roman Catholic and Protestant theological reflection on revelation. He concludes, though not surprisingly, given the deliberately ecumenical practice of *teología en* and *de conjunto* that characterizes the work of Latin@ theologians and biblical scholars, that Latin@ Roman Catholic and Protestant reflections on revelation "have much more in common than not."[8]

Gathering together the insights of the Latin@ thinkers whose contributions to theologies of revelation he considers, Agosto identifies several noteworthy common threads among them. The first is an emphasis on "the importance of culture, in this case Latino/a culture, as a vehicle of divine revelation."[9] Second, Agosto correctly understands that for many Latin@ biblical scholars and theologians, "revelation must be described as a contextual act, not a matter of universality. God chooses to reveal God-self in particularities, not absolute abstraction."[10] For the Latin@ scholars whose contributions Agosto reviews, "The experience of divine transcendence in human life—indeed, daily life, *lo cotidiano*—counts more than a delineation of the attributes of God that tend to distance God from human experience."[11]

---

[7] Agosto, "Revelation," 91.

[8] Agosto, "Revelation," 106.

[9] Agosto, "Revelation," 106. See Miguel H. Díaz, ed., *The Word Became Culture* (Maryknoll, NY: 2020), the first volume in the series, Disruptive Cartographers: Doing Theology Latinamente.

[10] Agosto, 106.

[11] Agosto, 106. On the place of *lo cotidiano*, lived daily experience, in Latin@ theologies, see Carmen M. Nanko-Fernández, "Lo Cotidiano as Locus Theologicus," in *The Wiley Blackwell Companion to Latino/a Theology*, ed. Orlando O. Espín (Malden, MA: Wiley Blackwell, 2015), 15–33.

Third, Agosto emphasizes that, for Latin@ theologians, "the incarnation of Christ, the ultimate statement of divine revelation in Christian theology and Scripture, is about embodiment."[12] Thus, embodiment figures prominently in Latin@ theologies, including theologies of revelation: "Any theology, including a theology of revelation, which incorporates *latinidad* engages matters of Latino/a identity, whether social, political, religious, national / ethnic, or the physical realities of gender and corporality, including *mestizaje* and *mulatez*."[13] Theologies that take embodiment seriously, Agosto goes on to say, must also involve ethical parameters. "We care about theology," he insists," because theology moves us—or should move us—to action."[14]

Although Agosto begins his essay on revelation by stating, "The starting point for a Latino/a theology of revelation is defining the expressions," and while the thumbnail definitions he cites come from non-Latin@ authors, in the end he makes it amply clear that the starting point is not a matter of trickle-down thinking from above, from the general to the more specific, but that quite the opposite is in fact the case when it comes to Latin@ approaches to revelation. Grounded in carefully nuanced understandings of *lo cotidiano* because they take the Incarnation seriously, Latin@ theologies underscore the significance of the particular without allowing this concern to lose its edge either by dissolving into individualism or by ascending beyond the clouds into ungrounded, inaccessible, and irrelevant abstraction.

While it would be hard to do justice to the carefully crafted argument of Rosario's *Dogmatics after Babel* here, this must-read book leads theology beyond the tension between what he calls the revelational approach associated with Karl Barth's "critical retrieval

---

12 Agosto, 107.
13 Agosto, 107.
14 Agosto, 107.

of orthodoxy" and the anthropological approach associated with
Paul Tillich's correlational approach.[15] Rosario correctly recognizes
the thinking of Barth and Tillich on the doctrine of revelation as
representing "two sides of the same coin, distinct in their methodologies, yet united in their overarching goal of resisting atheism and
secularization by providing uniquely Christian answers to Europe's
postwar woes."[16] Rosario goes on to offer a way past the impasse
by proposing a rich pneumatologically informed understanding of
revelation as sacramental encounter, an encounter with God that
is not restricted to the reading of sacred texts, but which is accessible in all of the places and all of the circumstances in which the
Spirit of God is active. Not only does Rosario argue that it is time
to move past narrow theologies of Word and Culture; the libera-
tionist pneumatological perspective that he offers demonstrates
convincingly how this is possible, yielding an understanding of
divine self-disclosure that is broad and deep.[17]

In his own contribution to *The Wiley Blackwell Companion
to Latino/a Theology*, an essay entitled "Sources and *En Conjunto*

---

[15] Rosario, *Dogmatics after Babel*, 31–32.

[16] Rosario, *Dogmatics after Babel*, 38.

[17] Rosario writes: "A focus on the work of the Spirit in human
history—especially through works of compassion and liberation—indicates
a possible strategy for moving past the impasse between the *theologies of
the Word* that take a fideistic stance on Scripture as God's self-revelation
without subjecting their dogmatic claims to external criticism, and the
theologies of culture that contend God can only be known through the
medium of culture but lack criteria for differentiating revelation from the
cultural status quo." Exploring the sacred texts of Judaism, Christianity,
and Islam, Rosario finds that "there exists a theological affirmation *within*
all three faiths that *wherever* the work of establishing justice, extending
compassion, and facilitating human liberation occurs, *there* is the true Spirit
of God. In effect, these emancipatory movements in history share in this
revelatory sacramental dimension because they embody the divine will for
all humankind regardless of confessional or creedal origin" (*Dogmatics after
Babel*, 175–76).

Methodologies of Latino/a Theologizing," Rosario understands that Latin@ theologians have managed to "avoid the dominant dichotomy between anthropological and revelational approaches" that he outlines in detail in *Dogmatics after Babel*. He also explains, first, that Latin@ theology

> identifies *revelation*—understood as God's self-revelation—as the primary sources of Christian theology. Specifically, the ultimate source of Christian faith and Christian doctrine is the man named Jesus, and what is known about him through the witness of the New Testament. Implied in this affirmation, however, is the recognition that the Scriptures are not the *unmediated* Word of God, but a *human* witness to the revelation of God in the man Jesus, called the Christ of God.[18]

Second, Rosario recognizes how Latin@ theologies affirm the role of culture as a source, explaining that revelation does not stand outside of or apart from culture, but that it takes place *within* culture. In that way, "there is no irreconcilable gap between God's act of self-revelation and humanity's capacity to understand and obey this revelation."[19] He cites with approval Orlando Espín's assertion that revelation, "in order to be claimed as revelation, must also be a human cultural event," noting that this makes the doctrine of the Incarnation central to Latin@ theology.[20]

[18] Rubén Rosario Rodríguez, "Sources and *En Conjunto* Methodologies of Latino/a Theologizing," in *The Wiley Blackwell Companion to Latino/a Theology*, ed. Orlando O. Espín (Malden, MA: Wiley Blackwell, 2015), 56.

[19] Rosario, "Sources," 56.

[20] Orlando O. Espín, *Idol and Grace: On Traditioning and Subversive Hope* (Maryknoll, NY: Orbis Books, 2014), 19, as quoted in Rosario, "Sources," 56. On incarnation, see Mayra Rivera, *The Poetics of the Flesh* (Durham, NC: Duke University Press, 2015).

By recommending the work of Agosto and Rosario on revelation in Latin@ theology, I can address what this book is not, and what this book does not attempt to do. Simply put: these pages do not attempt to outline a comprehensive theology of revelation. As I write these words, my eyes are drawn to the place on my bookshelf that is occupied by my well-worn copy of *Theology of Revelation* by René Latourelle, S.J., who was my professor in my first year of the first cycle in theology at the Pontifical Gregorian University. Originally published in French as *Théologie de la Révélation*, the English translation appeared in 1966, less than a year after the promulgation (on November 18, 1965) of the Second Vatican Council's Dogmatic Constitution on Divine Revelation (*Dei Verbum*).[21] Grateful as I am for what Latourelle taught me, it is not my intention to follow his example in this book.

As would be expected of a textbook by a professor at the Gregorian University of that era, Latourelle's five-hundred-page tome begins with a treatment of the biblical notion of revelation. Following that, he surveys revelation in the writings of the patristic period. Latourelle then goes on to treat revelation in the "theological tradition," a fairly selective presentation that includes the scholastics of the thirteenth century, scholastics after Trent, the scholastic "renewal" of the nineteenth century, and then the theology of revelation in the twentieth century. It is not surprising, given the vintage of the book, that Latourelle's treatment of "Protestant theology" in his historical survey is limited to a little more than one full page in his chapter on the twentieth century.[22] "Protestantism" receives just a bit more attention in the first chapter of part four of the book, which focuses on revelation and church magisterium. That chapter, entitled "The Council of Trent and

---

[21] René Latourelle, *Theology of Revelation, Including a Commentary on the Constitution "Dei Verbum" of Vatican II* (Staten Island, NY: Alba House, 1966).

[22] Latourelle, *Theology of Revelation*, 213–215.

Protestantism," occupies less than six pages.[23] That is followed by treatments of the First Vatican Council and its Dogmatic Constitution on the Catholic Faith (*Dei Filius*), a chapter on the Modernist Crisis, and a chapter on revelation during the pontificates of Pius XI and Pius XII.

The most valuable pages of Latourelle's *Theology of Revelation* are those he devotes to commentary on *Dei Verbum* only months after its promulgation, where, as a matter of considerable understatement, he observes that "the Constitution of Vatican II on revelation has not had a simple history."[24] At the safe distance of many years, I can confess with all due respect to the memory of my late professor, that it is only this section of the book, and in fact only the last two pages of text, that have remained as fresh in my recollection as the first day that I read them. There Latourelle points out the dramatic difference between the theocentric orientation of the First Vatican Council's Dogmatic Constitution on the Catholic Faith (*Dei Filius*) and the christocentric focus of *Dei Verbum*. At the beginning of chapter two of *Dei Filius*, we read, "It pleased his [*God's*] wisdom and goodness to reveal himself and the eternal decrees of his will in another and a supernatural way."[25] Chapter one of *Dei Verbum*, focused on revelation itself, begins, "In his goodness and wisdom, God chose to reveal himself and to make known to us the hidden purpose of his will by which *through Christ, the word made flesh*, man might in the Holy Spirit have

---

[23] Latourelle, *Theology of Revelation*, 249–254.

[24] Latourelle, *Theology of Revelation*, 484.

[25] First Vatican Council, Dogmatic Constitution on the Catholic Faith (*Dei Filius*), 2, as found in Heinrich Denzinger, *Compendium of Creeds, Definitions, and Declarations on Matters of Faith and Morals*, revised, enlarged, and, in collaboration with Helmut Hoping, ed. Peter Hünermann, Robert Fastiggi, and Anne Englund Nash (43d edition; San Francisco: Ignatius Press, 2012), §3004: "placuisse eius sapientiae et bonitati, alia eaque supernaturali via se ipsum ac aeternae voluntatis suae decreta humano generi revelare."

access to the Father and come to share in the divine nature" (*Dei Verbum* 2).[26] Though these portions of the two conciliar decrees both begin with similar references to God's goodness and wisdom, their differences could hardly be more dramatic. The narrowly propositional character of revelation in *Dei Filius* gives way to a relational understanding in *Dei Verbum*, where the goal of divine self-disclosure is to offer human beings access to the Father and a share in the divine nature. This is mediated, *Dei Verbum* explains, "through Christ, the Word made flesh." The importance of the Incarnation in Latin@ theologies, together with an understanding of divine self-disclosure as relational, very clearly reflects the emphases of *Dei Verbum*.

While reflection on the incarnation of the Word is a unifying thread throughout this book, the scope of my work in these pages is considerably less ambitious than Latourelle's.[27] I write as a biblical scholar and not as a systematic theologian, and my concern for theologies of revelation flows from a long-standing interest in translation.[28] Without setting aside my long-standing interest in the Revelation to John and the preoccupation with *apokalypsis* which that entails, I have long been fascinated by the Prologue of the Fourth Gospel, and so it should come as no surprise that I

---

[26] "Placuit Deo in sua bonitate et sapientia seipsum relevare et notum facere sacramentum voluntatis suae, quo homines, *per Christum, Verbum carnem factum*, in Spiritu Sancto accessum habent ad Patrem et divinae naturae consortes efficiuntur" (Denzinger, §4202).

[27] The scope of this book is also considerably more modest than the work of Gerald O'Collins, S.J., another professor of mine at the Gregorian. See Gerald O'Collins, *Revelation: Towards a Christian Interpretation of God's Self-Revelation in Jesus Christ* (Oxford, UK: Oxford University Press, 2016); idem, *Incarnation* (London, UK: Continuum, 2002).

[28] On the relationship between biblical scholars and theologians, see Jean-Pierre Ruiz, "Good Fences and Good Neighbors: Biblical Scholars and Theologians," in *Readings from the Edges*, 13–23.

began my initial foray into a Latin@ theology of revelation with two quotations, one from Václav Havel's acceptance speech on receiving the 1989 Peace Prize of the German Booksellers' Association, "Words about Words," and a second from Johann Wolfgang von Goethe's *Faust*.[29] The latter is worth a reprise as I begin this more extended consideration of revelation in these pages, insofar as it helps to begin unpacking what I mean by entitling this book *Revelation in the Vernacular*:

> For things above the earth we learn to pine,
> Our spirits yearn for revelation,
> Which nowhere burns with purer beauty blent,
> Than here in the New Testament.
> To ope the ancient text an impulse strong
> Impels me, and its sacred lore,
> With honest purpose to explore,
> And render into my loved German tongue.
> (*He opens a volume and applies himself to it.*)
> 'Tis writ, "In the beginning was the Word!"
> I pause, perplex'd! Who now will help afford?
> I cannot the mere Word so highly prize;
> I must translate it otherwise,
> If by the spirit guided as I read.
> "In the beginning was the Sense!" Take heed,
> The import of this primal sentence weigh,
> Lest thy too hasty pen be led astray!
> Is force creative then of Sense the dower?
> "In the beginning was the Power!"
> Thus should it stand: yet, while the line I trace

---

[29] Václav Havel, "Words on Words," Václav Havel Library Foundation, https://www.vhlf.org/havel-archives/words-on-words/.

A something warns me, once more to efface.
The spirit aids! From anxious scruples freed,
I write, "In the beginning was the Deed!"[30]

Here Goethe's protagonist "wrestles mightily with the translation of the first verse of the first chapter of John's Gospel. . . . 'In the beginning was the Word' fails to satisfy. Likewise, 'In the beginning was the Sense' (German *Sinn*, which can be rendered as 'sense' or 'meaning') falls short. . . . Finally, it is only 'In the beginning was the Deed' that constitutes a satisfying rendering."[31] Although theologians take considerable pains to distinguish between "general" and "special" revelation, I would argue that revelation is always particular, that divine self-disclosure takes place in the vernacular, even in the complex particularities of countless vernaculars.

"Vernacular" is a strange word. I first heard it in elementary school, when one day the wonderful Sister of Charity who was my teacher explained that henceforth the Mass would be celebrated "in the vernacular" rather than in Latin, and that something called "Vatican II" was somehow to blame for this. Good little Catholic boy though I was, at the time I had no clue about what she meant by "Vatican II," and "vernacular" was even more perplexing. It did not help at all when, only a few weeks later, Sister told us that we should no longer refer to the third person of the Trinity as the "Holy Ghost," and that we should use "Holy Spirit" instead. That was no big deal in my household though, because we were accustomed to invoking el Espiritu Santo or le Saint-Esprit and "Holy Ghost" had always sounded a little strange to us. As for "vernacular," we soon learned that this simply meant that Mass would be celebrated in English. It would be several more years before my mother very easily convinced our newly assigned Korean immi-

---

30 As quoted in Ruiz, "The Word Became Flesh," 48.
31 Ruiz, "The Word Became Flesh," 61.

grant associate pastor that our parish needed a Mass in Spanish and that he should be the presider and homilist!

Digging a bit deeper, according to Merriam-Webster, "vernacular" is a noun that means "an expression or mode of expression that occurs in ordinary speech rather than formal writing," or "the mode of expression of a group or class," or "a common name of a plant or animal as distinguished from the Latin nomenclature of scientific classification: a vernacular name of a plant or animal." Etymologically, it comes from the Latin *vernaculus*, "belonging to the household, domestic, native."[32] As for where my elementary school teacher found the word, only much later did I learn that it was used in the Second Vatican Council's Constitution on the Sacred Liturgy (*Sacrosanctum Concilium*).[33]

Curiously, though, "vernacular" is not used at all in the Council's Dogmatic Constitution on Divine Revelation (*Dei Verbum*).[34] The word does appear (twice) in *Divino Afflante Spiritu*,

---

[32] "Vernacular." *Merriam-Webster.com Dictionary*, Merriam-Webster, https://www.merriam-webster.com/dictionary/vernacular.

[33] The document states that "the use of the Latin language is to be preserved in the Latin rites. But since the use of the mother tongue, whether in the Mass, the administration of the sacraments, or other parts of the liturgy, frequently may be of great advantage to the people, the limits of its employment may be extended. This will apply in the first place to the readings and directives, and to some of the prayers and chants, according to the regulations on this matter to be laid down separately in subsequent chapters. These norms being observed, it is for the competent territorial ecclesiastical authority . . . to decide whether, and to what extent, the *vernacular language* [*linguae vernaculae*] is to be used." Second Vatican Council, Constitution on the Sacred Liturgy (*Sacrosanctum Concilium*), No. 36, https://www.vatican.va/archive/hist_councils/ii_vatican_council/documents/vat-ii_const_19631204_sacrosanctum-concilium_en.html.

[34] In chapter six, which attends to the place of Sacred Scripture in the life of the Church, we find: "Easy access to Sacred Scripture should be provided for all the Christian faithful. That is why the Church from the very beginning accepted as her own that very ancient Greek translation of

the 1943 encyclical of Pius XII on promoting biblical studies that set into motion the trajectory that led to *Dei Verbum*.[35] The first occurrence is a reference to Pius X, who in a January 1907 letter to Cardinal Francesco di Paola Cassetta praised the Society of St. Jerome's practice of promoting reading of and meditation on the Gospels, "proclaiming it 'a most useful undertaking, as well as most suited to the times,' seeing that it helps in no small way 'to dissipate the idea that the Church is opposed to or in any way impedes the reading of the Scriptures in the vernacular'" (*Divino Afflante Spiritu*, No. 9). The second occurrence is in the context of the pope's words of praise for the work of biblical scholars: "Many of them also, by the written word, have promoted and do still promote, far and wide, the study of the Bible; as when they edit the sacred text corrected in accordance with the rules of textual criticism or expound, explain, and translate it into the vernacular" (*Divino Afflante Spiritu*, No. 10).

Charting This Book

Maps are never neutral, and the making of maps is always a task that says as much about the cartographer as it does about the terrain that is charted, as Carmen Nanko-Fernández, Gary Riebe-Estrella, and Miguel H. Díaz suggest in their preface to this series.

---

the Old Testament which is called the septuagint; and she has always given a place of honor to other Eastern translations and Latin ones especially the Latin translation known as the vulgate. But since the word of God should be accessible at all times, the Church by her authority and with maternal concern sees to it that suitable and correct translations are made into different languages, especially from the original texts of the sacred books." *Dei Verbum* No. 22, http://www.vatican.va/archive/hist_councils/ii_vatican_council/documents/vat-ii_const_19651118_dei-verbum_en.html.

[35] Pope Pius XII, *Divino Afflante Spiritu*, September 30, 1943, https://www.vatican.va/content/pius-xii/en/encyclicals/documents/hf_p-xii_enc_30091943_divino-afflante-spiritu.html

The chapters of this book reflect the cardinal points of the series, with its charge to the disruptive cartographers involved in this project, first, to retrieve sources from a historical tradition that is complex, sources for theologizing that have too often been overlooked and that have therefore remained untapped. Second, and also in keeping with the spirit of this series, this work seeks to understand and contextualize these sources through distinctively Latin@ optics. It incorporates insights of present-day scholars within and beyond the disciplinary borders of theology, as well as from the legacy of theological reflection from the Iberian Peninsula and from the Americas that is bound up with the long and non-innocent history of colonization. Third, because doing theology *latinamente* privileges lived daily experience in its concreteness, this book considers what differences the understanding of revelation articulated in these pages might make in advancing a genuinely catholic understanding of divine self-disclosure in the present day.

The first chapter begins not on Patmos, the island in the Aegean Sea not far from the Turkish coast that toward the end of the first century CE provided a vantage point from which a seer named John addressed his Apocalypse to Jesus followers who lived in cities of what was the Roman province of Asia. It begins instead on another island with more than five centuries of colonial entanglements, Mona Island in the Caribbean, located east of the Dominican Republic and west of Puerto Rico. Now uninhabited, it was the site of important encounters at the end of the fifteenth century between the indigenous Taíno population and the Spanish colonizers. This chapter, entitled *"Plura Fecit Deus,"* explores what happened when Spanish colonizers made their way deep into the island's many caves and found there an abundance of indigenous images and symbols carved into the stone. Remarkably, they did not deface or destroy them, as so many of their contemporaries did when they encountered indigenous texts throughout the Americas. Instead, recognizing the importance of these markings, they added

Christian symbols of their own, along with inscriptions in Latin and in Spanish that succinctly express what they thought of what they beheld in the caves. Among these inscriptions is "*Plura Fecit Deus*," "God made many," a remarkable expression of their recognition of the breadth of the Creator's activity to which the Taíno glyphs provided vivid testimony, even if they did not fully grasp the symbolism of what they saw.

Chapter two is entitled "*Verbum Caro Factum Est:* The Vernacular and the Incarnation," quoting Vulgate translation of the first words of John 1:14, which is another of the inscriptions left behind by the sixteenth-century Spanish visitors to the caves deep below the then-inhabited surface of Mona Island. Inscribed anonymously in the stone of the cave wall, these words might be understood, on the one hand, as a Christian counterclaim over against the Taíno glyphs that its author beheld. They can also be understood, on the other hand, as a commentary on the catholicity of the Incarnation of the Word, a reflection on what the Spanish visitor may even have recognized not as idolatry but perhaps even as testimony to divine self-disclosure in an indigenous idiom found in a most unexpected location. This chapter, which also involves retrieval, turns to the life and the writings of the Augustinian Fray Luis de León (1527–1597), the eminent poet, humanist, and theologian who was a luminary of the *Siglo de Oro*, the Golden Age of Spanish literature. His translation of portions of the Bible (the Song of Songs in particular) into Spanish got him into trouble with the Inquisition, resulting in his imprisonment from March 1572 until December 1576. When he was finally acquitted of the charges against him, it is said that he returned to the podium at the University of Salamanca and began his lecture with, "As we were saying yesterday."

Fray Luis de León is important for this study because, as Colin P. Thompson explains, in the prologue to his commentary on the Song of Songs, "Fray Luis makes clear his incarnational view of

the language of the Bible."[36] There the learned Augustinian writes
that "the care the Holy Spirit takes to be conformed to our style
by copying our language and by imitating the whole range of our
mind and our condition is a wonderful thing."[37] I am not by any
means claiming that Luis de León's thinking about the Incarnation of the Word influenced the anonymous Spanish author of
the Johannine inscription on Mona Island either directly or even
remotely. What I do suggest in chapter two is that Luis de León's
work as a translator and the prominence of the Incarnation of the
Word in his thinking offer the beginnings of a theology of the
vernacular in sixteenth-century Spain. His understanding of revelation as a matter of divine communication that is conformed to the
"whole range of our mind and our condition" ("*toda la variedad de
nuestro ingenio e condiciones*") offers a suggestive set of optics from
sixteenth-century Spain through which to consider the two Latin-
language inscriptions I have mentioned, which archaeologists
have dated to the sixteenth century, as richly theological responses
to the indigenous glyphs. The two Latin-language inscriptions,
"*plura fecit Deus*," and "*Verbum caro factum est*," frame the Taíno
cave petroglyphs in positive terms that are drawn from the distinctively Christian language of the Spaniards who visited the caves,
in terms of a hermeneutical vocabulary that was current—though
highly controversial—in sixteenth-century Spain. In 1907 Pope
Pius X may have wanted "to dissipate the idea that the Church is
opposed to or in any way impedes the reading of the Scriptures in
the vernacular," yet that intention reflects his embarrassment by

---

[36] Colin P. Thompson, *The Strife of Tongues: Fray Luis de León and the
Golden Age of Spain* (Cambridge: Cambridge University Press, 1988), 27.

[37] "Es cosa maravillosa el cuidado que pone el Espíritu Santo en
conformarse con nuestro estilo, remedando nuestro lenguaje, e imitando
en sí toda la variedad de nuestro ingenio e condiciones." As cited in and
translated by Thompson, *The Strife of Tongues*, 27. On the Incarnation in
the thought of Fray Luis, see Thompson, *The Strife of Tongues*, 172–176.

regretful historical hindsight that such opposition had often been vigorously enforced in the past.

Like chapter one, chapter two of this book involves a retrieval of sources that have not typically informed thinking around theologies of revelation even in Latin@ theologies. Both chapters would run the risk of being relegated to the sidelines as esoteric but ultimately irrelevant academic exercises in sixteenth-century historical theology if it were not for the "So what?" component that is integral to this series. Taking up the mapping metaphor, this study would remain an antiquarian exercise in sixteenth-century Iberian and colonial cartography if it did not also aim to take advantage of insights that these sources offer to remap—even if only in part—a theology of revelation that is relevant for the twenty-first century.

In the light of that concern, chapter three, "From the Amazon to the Tiber: Words Incarnate in the World," begins with a discussion of the YouTube video in which Alexander Tschugguel explains "why we threw the Pachamama idols into the Tiber river."[38] In this well-publicized incident during the October 2019 Synod of Bishops for the Pan-Amazonian Region, wooden images that had been used in the October 4, 2019, consecration of the Synod to Saint Francis of Assisi in the Vatican Gardens and subsequently enshrined in the church of Santa Maria in Traspontina, were thrown into the Tiber, only to be recovered later by the *carabinieri*. Drawing on the final report of the 2019 Synod, this chapter maps the implications of a theology of revelation that takes the particularity of the Incarnation seriously not only as a singular and defining christological event but in terms not unlike those articulated by Fray Luis de León centuries ago. Quoting the 1992 *Santo Domingo Document* that was the result of the Fourth General Meeting of the Latin American and Caribbean Episcopate, Pope Francis wrote,

---

[38] "Why we threw the Pachamama idols into the Tiber river," https://youtu.be/1p74CEA1_go.

For the Church to achieve a renewed inculturation of the Gospel in the Amazon region, she needs to listen to its ancestral wisdom, listen once more to the voice of its elders, recognize the values present in the way of life of the original communities, and recover the rich stories of its peoples. In the Amazon region, we have inherited great riches from the pre-Columbian cultures. These include "openness to the action of God, a sense of gratitude for the fruits of the earth, the sacred character of human life and esteem for the family, a sense of solidarity and shared responsibility in common work, the importance of worship, belief in a life beyond this earth, and many other values." (*Querida Amazonia*, No. 70)[39]

Chapter four, " 'Seeds of the Word': A Latin American Cartography," begins by tracing the expression "seeds of the word" through the final documents of the General Conferences of CELAM from Aparecida in 2007, back to Santo Domingo in 1992, then back to Puebla in 1979, and to Medellín in 1968 where the expression was first employed by the Latin American bishops. Then I turn to consider the use of this expression in the documents of the Second Vatican Council from which the Latin American bishops drew their inspiration, and then to Justin Martyr, who coined the expression in the second century. Finally, I turn to consider the Postsynodal Exhortation of Pope Francis, *Querida Amazonia*.

During the pontificate of the first bishop of Rome from the Americas, and despite the misguided efforts of those who threw the Amazonian carvings into the Tiber, it can be said that the Amazon flowed into the Tiber, with the richness of the Amazonian

---

[39] Pope Francis, Postsynodal Apostolic Exhortation *Querida Amazonia*, February 2, 2020, https://www.vatican.va/content/francesco/en/apost_exhortations/documents/papa-francesco_esortazione-ap_20200202_querida-amazonia.html

vernaculars informing, enriching, and challenging the global church. Pope Francis wrote that:

> Everything that the Church has to offer must become incarnate in a distinctive way in each part of the world, so that the Bride of Christ can take on a variety of faces that better manifest the inexhaustible riches of God's grace. Preaching must become incarnate, spirituality must become incarnate, ecclesial structures must become incarnate. (*Querida Amazonia*, No. 6)

This repeated insistence on incarnation, I suggest, involves a significant rethinking of the notion of inculturation to the extent that we can say not only that the Word *became* culture but that the Word continues to *become* culture, revealed in countless vernaculars.[40] What is articulated in view of evangelization and inculturation opens up even more broadly and deeply in the direction of multilateral dialogue and *encuentro* that moves toward genuine *convivencia*. In the words of the final document of the Amazonian Synod, "The logic of the incarnation teaches that God, in Christ, is linked to human beings who belong to 'cultures peculiar to various peoples' (*Ad Gentes*, No. 9), and the Church, the People of God present among the peoples, has the beauty of a pluriform face rooted in many different cultures (cf. *Evangelii Gaudium*, No. 116)."[41] The words left behind by the anonymous

---

[40] Gerald O'Collins, among others, makes a distinction between "past (foundational) revelation and ongoing (dependent) revelation" (Gerald O'Collins, "Revelation Past and Present," in *Vatican II: Assessment and Perspectives Twenty-Five Years After (1962–1987)*, ed. René Latourelle [Mahwah, NJ: Paulist Press, 1988], 134).

[41] Synod of Bishops, Special Assembly for the Pan-Amazonian Region, *The Amazon: New Paths for the Church and for an Integral Ecology*, *Final Document*, October 26, 2019, No. 91, http://secretariat.synod.va/

Spanish visitor(s) to the caves of Mona Island, "*Plura fecit Deus*" and "*Verbum caro factum est*," together with the incarnational theology and the appreciation for the vernacular that nourished the efforts of Fray Luis de León as a translator of the Scriptures, echo insistently from the sixteenth century into the twenty-first in these words of the bishops of Amazonia. In this way the cartography of retrieval in which this book engages points forward in the direction of an expansive, open-ended, and still-developing mapping of divine self-disclosure in the many vernaculars of the twenty-first century. *Plura fecit Deus*!

---

content/sinodoamazonico/en/documents/final-document-of-the-amazon-synod.html

CHAPTER 1

PLURA FECIT DEUS

Colonial Encuentros on the Island of Mona

Mona Island (*Amona* in Taíno), only twenty-two square miles in area, and lying some forty miles west of Puerto Rico and thirty-eight miles east of the Dominican Republic, very rarely makes it into the news. The exception is when Cuban, Dominican, and Haitian migrants who seek to cross the treacherous waters of the Mona Passage, most often in fragile and overloaded wooden *yolas*, wind up stranded on its shores and apprehended by U.S. authorities.[1] Part of the Puerto Rican archipelago, Mona Island has been claimed by the U.S. since 1898, when, as a result of the Spanish–American war, Spain ceded Puerto Rico to the U.S., along with Guam and the Philippines, under the terms of the Treaty of Paris. Before becoming a U.S. possession, Puerto Rico had been a Spanish colony since 1493, when Christopher Columbus arrived there during the second of his four voyages. After four centuries under Spain's control and more than one hundred years of U.S.

---

[1] "Surge of migrants being smuggled to Puerto Rico," CBS This Morning Saturday, July 26, 2014, https://www.cbsnews.com/news/surge-of-migrants-being-smuggled-to-united-states-through-puerto-rico/. Juan Hernández, "Undocumented Cuban Migrants Reach Mona Island," *Caribbean Business*, December 29, 2015, https://caribbeanbusiness.com/undocumented-cuban-migrants-reach-mona-island/?cn-reloaded=1.

rule, Puerto Rico remains, as one author tellingly puts it, the oldest colony in the world.[2]

Now established as the *Reserva Natural Isla de Mona* (the Mona Island Nature Reserve), administered by Puerto Rico's *Departamento de Recursos Naturales y Ambientales* (the Department of Natural and Environmental Resources), the island is inhabited only by rangers who are responsible for overseeing the campers, the hunters, and the tourists who visit the island, and also by scientists who are engaged in research on the island's endemic flora and fauna. Together with its smaller neighbor islands Monita and Desecheo, Mona has been called "the Galapagos of the Caribbean." Although visiting the island requires a permit, the Discover Puerto Rico website tempts potential visitors to "Embark on a once in a lifetime adventure to an untouched Caribbean island. Imagine a trip to an uninhabited island where you can unplug from everyday life and connect to nature and yourself. On Mona Island . . . you can clear your mind with the rhythmic sounds of the gentle waves and breathe in the freshest air."[3]

This now-pristine island was not always uninhabited. When Christopher Columbus arrived there in 1494, "one or more indigenous communities lived on Mona's coast, a day's canoe journey from the neighbouring, larger islands, tending agricultural plots and taking advantage of the abundant terrestrial and marine resources."[4] The archaeological evidence indicates that the human

[2] José Trías Monge, *Puerto Rico: The Trials of the Oldest Colony in the World* (New Haven, CT: Yale University Press, 1997).

[3] "Exploring Mona Island," *Discover Puerto Rico*, https://www.discoverpuertorico.com/article/exploring-mona-island

[4] Jago Cooper, Alice V. M. Samson, Miguel A. Nieves, Michael J. Lace, Josué Caamaño-Dones, Caroline Cartwright, Patricia N. Kambesis, and Laura del Olmo Frese, "'The Mona Chronicle': The Archaeology of Early Religious Encounter in the New World," *Antiquity* 90, no. 352 (2016): 1055.

history of Mona Island began as early as 2800 BCE.[5] According to Ovidio Dávila Dávila, the indigenous presence on Mona ended in 1578, when the few remaining Taínos were relocated from the island to Puerto Rico on the initiative of Diego de Salamanca, the Bishop of Puerto Rico, out of his concern for the dire situation in which they found themselves.[6] In the decades between the arrival of the Spanish colonizers in 1494 and the departure of Mona's last indigenous inhabitants, the

---

[5] Alice V. M. Samson, Jago E. Cooper, Miguel A. Nieves, Lucy J. Wrapson, David Redhouse, Rolf-Martin Vieten, Osvaldo De Jesús Rullan, Tiana García López de Victoria, Alex Palermo Gómez, Victor Serrano Puigdoller, Delise Torres Ortiz, and Ángel Vega de Jesús, "Indigenous Cave Use, Isla de Mona, Puerto Rico," in *Proceedings of the 25th International Congress for Caribbean Archaeology* (San Juan, PR: Academia Puertorriqueña, 2015), 3.

[6] Ovidio Dávila Dávila, *Arqueología de la Isla de Mona* (San Juan, PR: Editorial Instituto de Cultura Puertorriqueña, 2003), 36. Dávila refers to a letter written by the bishop to the king of Spain in which he requested that the remaining inhabitants of Mona be relocated, expressing his concern that on Mona there remained "hasta 10 ó 12 hombres y mujeres, chicos y grandes, y no hay posibilidad de poderlos visitor ni doctrinarlos, aunque dicen ser cristianos y rezar, jamás se les dicen misa, ni puede saberse cómo viven (aunque se cree que no muy bien)." With respect to the word "Taíno," José R. Oliver explains how "it is worth remembering that the noun 'Taíno' ... is essentially a modern anthropological construct that glosses over significant sociocultural, political, economic, ethnic, and linguistic variability in the greater Antilles. Consistently, the early Spanish documents refer to the native populations as people of this Indies or as Indians of this 'island' or that 'territory.' Taíno derived from the noun used to designate elite individuals, nitaíno (/ni-taí-no or 'us-noble/good-persons) first reported in Columbus's second voyage in 1494 when a native was confronted with the question of 'who are you,'" ("The Proto-Taíno Monumental Cemís of Caguana," in *Ancient Borinquen: Archaeology and Ethnohistory of Ancient Puerto Rico*, ed. Peter E. Siegel (Tuscaloosa: University of Alabama Press, 2005), 281.

indigenous populations were fully immersed in direct contact with Europeans and Africans throughout the sixteenth century. This *indio* population experienced a generation of transformation as Spanish power was increasingly projected into the Caribbean. Islanders produced and exported agricultural products, especially cassava bread, and finished goods such as cotton shirts and hammocks for the first Spanish settlements, increasingly supplying food and water to European ships on their way to or from the Indies.[7]

As active as the interaction between the indigenous Taíno inhabitants of Mona and Europeans and Africans may have been on the island, evidence suggests that their subterranean interactions are even more remarkable. With its more than two hundred cave complexes, Mona Island has been described as one of the world's most cavernous places.[8]

Archaeologists note that "Indigenous presence has been identified in 30 cave systems around the island. Evidence includes the greatest diversity of preserved indigenous iconography in the Caribbean, with thousands of motifs recorded in darkzone chambers far from cave entrances."[9] Those who made these images used a variety of different techniques, "charcoal-based imagery, painted petroglyphs, etched geometric images . . . and figures or patterns

---

[7] Cooper et al., "'The Mona Chronicle,'" 1056. Also see Karen E. Anderson-Córdova, "The Aftermath of Conquest: The Indians of Puerto Rico during the Early Sixteenth Century," in *Ancient Borinquen*, 337–352.

[8] Cooper et al., "The Mona Chronicle," 1057. Also see Patricia Kambesis, "Documenting the Caves of Isla de Mona," *Espeleorevista Puerto Rico* 4 (January–June 2011): 4–7; as well as Michael J. Lace, "Anthropogenic Use, Modification, and Preservation of Coastal Cave Resources in Puerto Rico, *Journal of Island and Coastal Archaeology*, 7, no. 3 (2012): 384.

[9] Cooper et al., "'The Mona Chronicle,'" 1058.

lightly traced by hand or tool into the soft corrosion residues of accessible cave ceilings and walls."[10] These images include geometric designs, along with "extensive and complex imagery of anthrozoomorphic and ancestral beings (cemíes)."[11] The presence of such a high density of designs and pictographs in chambers that had no natural light and that were located at a considerable distance from the entrances to the caves suggests that both the images and the caves themselves had cultural significance that might be described as religious, and that these inaccessible chambers were not ordinarily used for the activities of daily life.[12]

Peter E. Siegel explains that "the Taíno worldview was based on a concentric model of the universe, with three distinct layers representing various planes of reality. The earthly plane, in the middle, was surrounded by a celestial vault above and subterranean waters below, with all three connected by sacred caves."[13] The importance of caves in Taíno cosmology was complemented by their significance in their story of human origins. Sebastián Robiou Lamarche writes that the Taínos believed that their ancestors came from the island they called *Ayiti* (which the Europeans named *la Española*, Hispaniola) an island they considered a living thing. Its

---

[10] Lace, "Anthropogenic Use," 385.

[11] Cooper et al., "'The Mona Chronicle,'" 1058. The term *cemí* or *zemí* (plural *cemíes* or *zemíes*) refers to Taíno deities and to representations of those deities. As Irving Rouse explains, "The term *zemi* was applied not only to the deities themselves but also to idols and fetishes representing them" (*The Taínos: Rise and Decline of the People Who Greeted Columbus* [New Haven, CT: Yale University Press, 1992], 13). Also see Peter E. Siegel, "Ancestor Worship and Cosmology among the Taíno," in *Taíno: Pre-Columbian Art and Culture from the Caribbean*, ed. Fatima Bercht, Estrellita Brodsky, John Alan Farmer, and Dicey Taylor (New York: El Museo del Barrio and Monacelli Press, 1997), 106–111.

[12] See Holley Moyes, ed., *Sacred Darkness: A Global Perspective on the Ritual Use of Caves* (Boulder: University Press of Colorado, 2012).

[13] Siegel, "Ancestor Worship and Cosmology among the Taíno," 108.

caves were regarded as a sort of uterus of Mother Earth from which creation emerged.[14] Several of these were of particular importance for the Taíno cosmogony. The first of these was Iguanaboína, the cave in the east from which the sun and the moon emerged. The first human beings emerged from two caves on a mountain called Cauta, which was located at the center of the island. According to Robiou Lamarche, this mountain, with its two caves, was considered the *axis mundi*, the cosmic center, with the Taínos originating from the cave on that mountain called Cacibajagua, and non-Taínos from the cave called Amayaúna. They believed that in the remote past, Cacibajagua had been inhabited by primal beings who could not stand the sunlight. When some of these beings emerged from the cave, the sun transformed them into the first Táinos. Another cave, Guacayarima, was located in the extreme western part of the island, and that cave served as the sun's entrance into the underworld, through which it passed at night only to rise once again from the east the following morning.[15]

When we take into consideration the vital symbolic significance of caves in the worldview of the indigenous peoples who had

[14] Sebastián Robiou Lamarche, *Taínos y Caribes: Las culturas aborígenes antillanas* (San Juan, PR: Editorial Punto y Coma, 2019), 85. Much of what Robiou Lamarche and others write about Taíno cosmology and other aspects of the Taíno worldview is drawn from the *Account of the Antiquities of the Indians*, completed in 1498 by Fray Ramón Pané, a Hieronymite priest who accompanied Columbus on his second voyage. See José Juan Arrom, *Fray Ramón Pané: An Account of the Antiquities of the Indians. A New Edition with an Introductory Study, Notes, and Appendixes*, translated by Susan C. Griswold (Durham, NC: Duke University Press, 1999). On Pané, see David Solodkow, "Fray Ramón Pané y el *Ego* evangelizador: Matrices etnográficas, violencia y ficcionalización del Otro," *Revista de estudios hispánicos* 42, no. 2 (2008): 237–259.

[15] Robiou Lamarche, *Taínos y Caribes*, 86–87; idem, *Mitología y religion de los Taínos* (San Juan, PR: Editorial Punto y Coma, 2006), 15–17. Also see Antonio M. Stevens-Arroyo, *The Cave of the Jagua* (Scranton, PA: University of Scranton Press, 2008), 138, 151–152.

inhabited Mona long before the arrival of the Europeans, it comes as no real surprise that the island's caves contain so many pictographs. As Jago Cooper and his colleagues suggest:

> The markings on the cave walls and extraordinary acoustic, olfactory and haptic properties of the environment offer a powerful experience of alterity, enhanced by the lack of usual sensory stimulation, disorientating and heightening awareness, and morphing perspectives of space and time. Hundreds of metres underground, torch or lamplight flickering across representations of *cemíes* on walls and ceilings, some reflected in pools of water, would have made a powerful impression on all visitors to the caves.[16]

To be sure, indigenous rock art is not limited to the caves of Mona. Indigenous pictographs and petroglyphs are widespread across Puerto Rico, and the earliest of these date to 600 CE. On the island of Puerto Rico they are found in caves, indigenous ball courts, on river boulders, and also on beaches.[17]

Peter Roe laments that Puerto Rican rock art has been "long known but little studied."[18] He asks, "Why study ancient Puerto Rican rock art?" Based on the nature of the evidence itself, he answers, "In contrast to the often fragmentary and disturbed nature of archaeological remains, rock art is usually found in situ and intact. Thus, it preserves both its original spatial context . . . and the cultural 'intent,' however veiled, of its original makers."[19] The convergence of spatial context and cultural intent, to the extent

---

[16]   Cooper et al., "'The Mona Chronicle,'" 1059.

[17]   See Peter G. Roe, "Rivers of Stone, Rivers within Stone: Rock Art in Puerto Rico," in *Ancient Borinquen*, 285–336. Also see Oliver, "The Proto-Taíno Monumental Cemís of Caguana," in *Ancient Borinquen*, 230–284.

[18]   Roe, "Rivers of Stone," 299.

[19]   Roe, "Rivers of Stone," 297.

that the latter can be assessed, is eminently clear with respect to the rock art that has been found in the caves of Mona Island. The study of indigenous rock art *per se* both in the caves on Mona Island and in various sites in Puerto Rico deserves more detailed attention than can be devoted to it here. Such considerations would be out of place in a book that seeks to chart a path through a Christian theology of revelation were it not for what British and Puerto Rican archaeologists and speleologists found between 2013 and 2016 when they explored one cave in particular. Their discoveries, part of the *Corazón del Caribe* research project, propelled Mona Island into the news with headlines like "Cave Walls Record Early Encounters between Old World and New," after the initial results of their work were published in 2016.[20] The leap from the pages of a somewhat obscure academic journal to a broader public in *National Geographic, Smithsonian, Newsweek,* and even Fox News was remarkable.

Encuentros in Cave Eighteen

Although formal archaeological research on Mona Island dates to 1952, and while it was in 1973 that Puerto Rican geographer

---

[20] See A. R Williams, "Cave Walls Record Early Encounters between Old World and New," *National Geographic,* July 19, 2016, https://www. nationalgeographic.com/history/article/cave-art-caribbean-mona-island-first-contact-archaeology; James Rogers, "Mysterious rock art uncovered in caves on uninhabited Caribbean island," *Fox News,* October 30, 2017; Hannah Osborne, "Rock Art Discovered in Deep Dark Caves Reveal Early Human Civilization on Puerto Rico's Uninhabited Mona Island," *Newsweek,* October 30, 2017, https://www.newsweek.com/ puerto-rico-mona-island-cave-art-early-humans-civilization-696239; Jason Daley, "Archaeologists Date Pre-Hispanic Puerto Rican Rock Art for the First Time," *Smithsonian Magazine,* November 2, 2017, https://www. smithsonianmag.com/smart-news/archaeologists-date-puerto-rican-rock-art-first-time-180967050/. Cooper et al., "'The Mona Chronicle.'"

Pedro Santana identified pre-Columbian rock art in several of the island's caves, it was not until the discoveries of the *el Corazón del Caribe* project were published in 2016 that the full significance of these images became evident.[21] When Jago Cooper and his colleagues reached Cave 18 on the island's southern coast and made their way some fifty meters past the entrance, they found that some "250 separate motifs, made by dragging one to four fingers ('finger-fluting'), and finger-sized tools through the soft deposits of the cave surfaces, cover the walls, ceilings and alcoves in 10 chambers and interconnecting tunnels over some 6500m²— about 15 per cent of the cave system."[22] In addition to this large trove of indigenous images, which they dated to the fourteenth and fifteenth centuries CE, the researchers found "More than 30 historic inscriptions in cave 18" including "phrases in Latin and Spanish, names, dates and Christian symbols that occur within a series of connecting chambers, all within the area of indigenous iconography."[23]

Of particular interest are three inscribed phrases, two of them in Latin and one in Spanish, all three of which they were able to date (by paleographic analysis) to the sixteenth century.[24] The first of these is *"Plura fecit deus,"* "God made many things." About this phrase, Cooper and his colleagues note:

---

[21] Alice V. M. Sampson and Jago Cooper, "History on Mona Island: Long-term Human and Landscape Dynamics of an 'Uninhabited' Island," *New West Indian Guide* 89 (2015): 39–40; Pedro M. Santana, *La Isla de Mona en los tempos precolombinos: Las Islas de Mona y Monito: Una evaluación de sus recursos naturales e históricos* (San Juan, PR: Junta de Calidad Ambiental, 1973).

[22] Cooper et al., "'The Mona Chronicle,'" 1060.

[23] Cooper et al., "'The Mona Chronicle,'" 1061.

[24] For a complete list of the European inscriptions, see Alice V. M. Samson, Jago Cooper, and Josué Caamaño-Dones, "European Visitors in Native Spaces: Using Paleography to Investigate Early Religious Dynamics in the New World," *Latin American Antiquity* 27, no. 4 (2016): 446–447.

There is no obvious contemporary textual source; the commentary appears to be a spontaneous response to whatever the visitor experienced in the cave. There is a strong spatial inference that "things" is a reference to the extensive indigenous iconography present. The phrase may express the theological crisis of the New World discovery, throwing the personal human experience and reaction into sharp relief.[25]

A second Latin inscription is "*Verbum caro factum est*," "the Word was made flesh," the first part of John 1:14 according to the Vulgate translation. Cooper and his fellow researchers assume that "this well-known chapter of the Bible would have been familiar even to Christians without formal Latin education."[26] While that is probably true, we will see that this inscription, along with the first, is key to understanding how the European visitors to Cave 18 made sense of what they saw there against the backdrop of their own Iberian Christian context. Of the three inscriptions, only this one is accompanied by a name on a line just below the inscription, possibly even the name of the person who wrote it, a certain "Bernardo" about whom nothing else is known.[27]

A third inscription, this one in Spanish, is "*Dios te perdone*," "May God forgive you." Commenting on these words, Cooper and his colleagues note,

This is a common Christian petition, which implies a separation between the author and the subjects, or acts that require forgiveness, and the intercessional role of the author, perhaps akin to a confessional pardon between

---

[25] Cooper et al., "'The Mona Chronicle,'" 1062.

[26] Cooper et al., "'The Mona Chronicle,'" 1062.

[27] Samson et al., "European Visitors to Native Spaces," 450.

priest and sinner. Another implication is that the attendant practices, now invisible to us, require forgiveness as well as the images themselves.[28]

Common though the expression may be, and accurate though it may also be that it implies a separation between the author and the acts or the persons that the author regards as in need of forgiveness, it may be one step too far to liken it to "a confessional pardon between priest and sinner," since sacramental absolution would not have been conferred in writing. Whatever the case may have been, though, this third phrase represents a substantially different—and less sympathetic—response to the indigenous cave art on the part of the European visitor who wrote it than did the two Latin inscriptions found in Cave 18. Not everyone among the European visitors arrived at the same conclusion when they came face to face with the Taíno pictographs!

Along with these inscriptions, Cave 18 also contains numerous Christian symbols, among them two depictions of Calvary, one of which depicts three crosses, with the central cross captioned "Iesus." The second consists of two crosses, inscribed so that they "flank an indigenous anthropomorphic figure," so that "this triptych has clear compositional parallels with representations of Calvary in which the central figure is strikingly cast as an indigenous Jesus."[29] Remarkably, this iconography, whether intentionally or not, gives graphic expression to the intuitions that are expressed not too far away in the same cave by the two Latin inscriptions *Plura fecit Deus*, and *Verbum caro factum est*. Is it possible that this might depict an indigenous Jesus? Could it possibly suggest a wideness to the notion of the Incarnation that included (or at least that did not exclude) indigenous humanity?

---

[28] Cooper et al., "'The Mona Chronicle,'" 1062.

[29] Cooper et al., "'The Mona Chronicle,'" 1063–1064.

The researchers also report finding "a series of 17 crosses" in the cave, "ranging from simple Latin crosses to more complex Calvary crucifixes," and that these are located "most often close to indigenous finger-fluting and iconography." The placement of these crosses is significant. According to the researchers, "Crosses are placed in visually dominant positions over cave entrances or on high walls, most being set vertically above indigenous iconography rather than superimposed. This vertical ordering is a clear and cross-culturally understood visual convention of hierarchical relations."[30] This is an important and, in all likelihood, an accurate assessment of the symbolic rhetoric that was deployed in this cave to claim the superiority of the Christian worldview to that represented by the symbols that were drawn from the indigenous visual lexicon. Yet it is equally significant that the crosses were not superimposed over the indigenous iconography, nor is there evidence that any of the indigenous iconography were defaced or erased by those who were responsible for making the crosses. In at least one case in Cave 18, a cross has been incised into a niche so that it faces the incised image of an indigenous ancestral figure that is directly across from it, presenting a visual disputation of sorts, a contest of meanings, between the Taíno pictograph and the Christian symbol.[31] Even so, the Taíno image was not vandalized in any way.

Researchers also documented the presence of a variety of Christograms in Cave 18, the traditional abbreviation of Jesus or of Christ, including *IHS* (the first three Greek letters of the name of Jesus, *iota- ēta-sigma*) and *IHS* followed by a cross and then followed by *XRS* (*chi-rho-sigma*). The letter *ēta* of these Christograms, they note, has a cross through its vertical line, a not uncommon stylistic practice of the time. Thus, "The name of

---

[30] Cooper et al., "'The Mona Chronicle,'" 1064.

[31] Cooper et al., "'The Mona Chronicle,'" 1068, figure 12.

Christ engraved into the walls of the cave materialises a Christian characterisation of the space."[32]

The sixteenth-century Spanish visitors to Cave 18 were not all anonymous. Besides the inscriptions and the images they left behind, and besides the "Bernardo" who added his name below *Verbum caro factum est*, several of them also wrote their names and the year they visited: Myguel Rypoll (1550), Alonso Pérez Roldan el Mozo (1550 August), and Alonso de Contreras (1554). One visitor to the cave, Francisco Alegre, is recognized from archival records as a prominent Spanish official in Puerto Rico during the sixteenth century, whose responsibilities included oversight of the crown's estates, including Mona Island.[33] Besides these figures who identified themselves by their names, another inscription identifies an unnamed canon—an ecclesiastical official—among the mid-sixteenth-century European visitors to the cave.

Why did these Europeans visit Cave 18 and how did they find it? Unfortunately, none of the evidence they left behind gives us anything that allows for a straightforward answer. What we do know is that there was significant interaction between the European colonizers and the indigenous Taínos on the island. Valuable evidence that their interactions were not limited to the production and export of agricultural products and other goods is provided in a letter addressed to the king of Spain by Bishop Rodrigo de Bastidas (ca. 1497–1570). He reported about the five or six days he spent on Mona that he found its indigenous inhabitants to be "truly Christian," and that they had a church in which they gathered twice a day, in the morning and in the

---

[32] Cooper et al., "'The Mona Chronicle,'" 1065. The researchers also suggest how "the dominance of the Christ figure (as opposed to Mary or another saint) confers a Christocentric devotional character that was rooted in late medieval tradition and became increasingly popular in New World shrines throughout the sixteenth and seventeenth centuries" (1065).

[33] Cooper et al., "'The Mona Chronicle,'" 1065.

evening. Before leaving, he heard their confessions, and baptized and confirmed their children.[34]

Evidence like this, according to Cooper and his colleagues, "suggests that indigenous Christians were themselves directly engaged with this arrival of a new ideology and associated visual culture. It is possible that some of the finger-drawn crosses in cave 18 may have been executed by *indios conversos* (indigenous peoples converting to Christianity), as has been proposed for the colonial Andes." They leave open to further study the question of "whether at least some of the historic inscriptions and names may belong to indigenous individuals."[35] Even if it was the case that some of the sixteenth-century visitors to Cave 18 were indigenous Christians, at least some of the others were "elite males of Spanish ancestry, knowledgeable about certain aspects of indigenous culture, conversant with indigenous beliefs and willing to engage with them."[36] While these visitors might have happened on Cave 18 on their own, it is far more likely that they learned of it from Taínos—possibly even Christian Taínos—who lived on the island, and who may even have shown them the way.

Why would these Europeans have visited Cave 18, either alone or in the company of indigenous residents of Mona (Christian or

---

[34] Archivo General de Indias, Audiencia de Santo Domingo, 172, no. 14, letter of Bishop Rodrigo de Bastidas, September 1, 1548, as cited in Dávila Dávila, *Arqueología de la Isla de Mona*, 33: "Yo visité la Isla de la Mona y estuve en ella cinco o seis días. Vine muy consolado de ver unos pocos indios que en ella están, todos los más casados, y certifico a V.M. que, a lo que alcancé, verdaderamente cristianos y que sienten del cristianismo como tales. Tienen una iglesia con su pobreza ataviada, en la cual se juntan dos veces al día, a la mañana y a la tarde, a decir la doctrina cristiana. Déjelos todos confesados y bautizados y confirmados todos los niños, y con todo esto consolados."

[35] Cooper et al., "'The Mona Chronicle,'" 1066.

[36] Cooper et al., "'The Mona Chronicle,'" 1067.

otherwise), not just once, but on multiple occasions?[37] Cooper and his colleagues propose three suggestions. The first is very pragmatic: fostering harmonious relationships would have been to the mutual economic and political advantage of both the indigenous population of Mona and the island's colonizers. Second, they speculate that "the construction of new colonial landscapes may have been related to the emergence of an *indio converso* identity," a developing identity that was the result of missionary activity on Mona. The letter of Bishop Rodrigo de Bastidas and the existence of a church on Mona in the middle of the sixteenth century, a church that was frequented by the island's Taíno inhabitants, strongly supports this. Third, "from a coloniser perspective, the founding of local Christian shrines was essential to carving out a local Caribbean identity, drawing on indigenous traditions, in line with a post-reformation trend for shrine formation."[38]

The practice of repurposing existing sacred spaces and shrines has a long, rich, and complex history in Christianity. One need only think of the Pantheon, first built as a temple to Roman gods and subsequently consecrated (in 609 CE) as the Church of Santa Maria ad Martyres. In Córdoba, a Roman era temple to the god Janus was repurposed into a church by the Visigoths in the sixth century, only to be repurposed by Abd al-Rahman I into a masjid, which was then once again repurposed into a church during the *Reconquista*. In the Americas, perhaps the best-known repurposing of this sort took place in Mexico on the hill of Tepeyac. Where the Nahua goddess Tonantzin had been venerated, a Christian church was built to commemorate the Virgin Mary's appearances at that site in 1531, honoring her request that a church be built there in her honor. This, of course, is the story of Our Lady of Guadalupe.[39]

---

[37] Cooper et al., "'The Mona Chronicle,'" 1066.
[38] Cooper et al., "'The Mona Chronicle,'" 1066.
[39] See David A. Sánchez, *From Patmos to the Barrio: Subverting Impe-*

As Cooper and his co-authors suggest, this offers at least one prom-
ising explanation for the presence of sixteenth-century Christian
images and inscriptions in Cave 18 on Mona Island, where so many
indigenous pictographs were also present that predated them.
What was, in effect, an indigenous subterranean sacred space was
repurposed as a Christian shrine, and yet without either defacing or
erasing the indigenous images that were already there.

That is what is so remarkable about what happened—or did
not happen—in Cave 18. It was certainly not typical of Spanish
colonial policies and practices with regard to indigenous symbols
and images. In his study of Andean indigenous rock art, José Luis
Martínez C. explains how one sixteenth-century viceroy, expressed
concern that by observing their custom of painting "idols and
images of animals and demons," the people were holding on to
their "old idolatry." He therefore forbade the making of such
images under the pain of severe punishment, ordering that these
images be removed from homes and other buildings when possible,
and replaced with crosses.[40]

---

rial Myths (Minneapolis: Fortress Press, 2008), chap. 2, "Subverting a
Conquista Myth in Seventeenth-Century Mexico: The Virgin of Guadalupe" (47–82).

  [40] José Luis Martínez C., "Registros Andinos al margen de la escritura:
el arte rupestre colonial," *Boletin del Museo Chileno de Arte Precolombino* 14
(2009): 9: "Item, porque de la costumbre envejecida que los indios tienen
de pintar ídolos y figuras de demonios y animales a quien solian mochar
en sus dúhos, tianas, vasos, báculos, paredes y edificios, mantas, camisetas,
lampas y casi en todas cuantas cosas les son necesarias, parece que en alguna
manera conservan su antigua idolatría, proveereis, en entrando en cada
repartimiento, que ningún oficial de aquí en adelante labre ni pinte las
tales figuras so graves penas, las cuales executareis en sus personas y bienes,
lo contrario haciendo. Y las pinturas y figuras que tuvieren en sus casas y
edificios y en los demás instrumentos que buenamente y sin mucho daño
se pudieren quitar y señalareis que se pongan cruces y otras insignias de
xptianos en sus casas y edificios."

The tragic but altogether too frequent practice of burning indigenous books during the colonial period is well known and amply documented. For example, in his 1566 *Relación de las cosas de Yucatán*, the Franciscan Fray Diego de Landa wrote, "We found a great number of these books in Indian characters, and because they contained nothing but superstition and the Devil's falsehoods, we burned them all; and this they felt most bitterly and it caused them great grief."[41] At the same time, in his *Historia de las Indias de Nueva España e Islas de la Tierra Firme* (1581) the Dominican Fray Diego Durán complained about those who had burned the indigenous books, not because he recognized or respected their inherent value, but because it made the work of Christianizing the indigenous population more difficult. He writes:

> Those who with fervent zeal (though with little prudence) in the beginning burned and destroyed all the ancient Indian pictographic documents were mistaken. They left us without a light to guide us—to the point that the Indians worship idols in our presence, and we understand nothing of what goes on in their dances, in their market-places, in their bath-houses, in the songs they chant (when they lament their ancient gods and lords), in their repasts and banquets; these things mean nothing to us.[42]

In Durán's estimation, the indigenous books would have been worth preserving because he believed they contained the code that he and his fellow missionaries would need to decipher the religious practices of those who were the object of their efforts at evangelization. Without these books, he complained, the people "worshipped

---

[41] As cited in Tzvetan Todorov, *The Conquest of America: The Question of the Other*, trans. Richard Howard (Norman: University of Oklahoma Press, 1999), 200.

[42] As cited in Todorov, *The Conquest of America*, 203.

idols" in their presence while they remained clueless about the significance of what was going on right in front of them.

Durán also complained about another book-burning but for a remarkably different reason. Todorov notes that, on the one hand, Durán was "a rigid, intransigent Christian, defender of religious purity," while on the other hand he was "quite willing to indulge in analogy and comparison in order to make the Mexican realities intelligible" to his presumably European reader, to the point of "discovering the essential rites of the Christian religion 'exactly' reproduced in the Aztec ritual."[43] Todorov explains how Durán "heard that the Indians in one village possessed a book written in characters they did not understand." On arriving there, he is disappointed to find out that the book had been burned, and so he writes, "I was sorry to hear this, because the manuscript could have shed light on our suspicion that it might have been the Holy Gospel in Hebrew. Vehemently I reprehended those who had had the book burned."[44]

With regard to the attitude of the Spanish colonizers toward Taíno religious images, Peter Martyr of Anghiera (1457–1526), the Italian historian who was appointed chronicler for the Council of the Indies, wrote of the Taínos and their *cemíes*: "All have been already subjugated by the Christians and without exception the obstinate ones are dead, without any trace of the *zemes* [cemíes], which have been taken to Spain so that we could understand the

---

[43] Todorov, *The Conquest of America*, 207, 208.

[44] Todorov, *The Conquest of America*, 209. It should be remembered, though, that the European colonizers were not the only ones who burned books. Elizabeth Hill Boone explains that when Bernardino de Sahagún's indigenous informants were telling of an event in the distant Mexica past, they told him, "'No longer can it be remembered, no longer can it be investigated how long they [the Mexica] were left in Tamoanchan' because the ruler Itzcoatl [*1427–1440 CE*] later burned the history books and destroyed the memory of it" (*Stories in Red and Black: Pictorial Histories of the Aztecs and Mixtecs* [Austin: University of Texas Press, 2000], 20.

effrontery and deceit of their devils."[45] Even Bartolomé de las Casas expressed similarly negative views of Taíno religious practices as demonic, writing that they

> Did not have idols, only rarely, and then not for worship, but only to be used imaginatively by certain priests used by the devil. . . . They did not have external or visible ceremonies, but only a few, and these were conducted by those priests whom the devil appointed as his ministers.[46]

Luis N. Rivera points out, though, that elsewhere in his writings, las Casas "develops a more complex vision of Indian idolatry with three components: (a) it comes from the inherent human impulse to know and venerate God (natural inclination to latria); (b) that impulse toward the divine is distorted by the perverse action of devils (becoming idolatry); (c) this parody of authentic worship become embedded by custom."[47] Rivera goes on to explain that las Casas "makes a theologically interesting remark that he, however, does not develop: the American natives initially 'had a special knowledge of the true God'—he does not say how they arrived at it—'and they went to him with his sacrifices, worship, and veneration.'"[48] From this path, las Casas laments, Satan led them astray.[49]

The early encounters between the indigenous peoples of the Americas and their European colonizers were not always as

---

[45] As quoted in Luis N. Rivera, *A Violent Evangelism: The Political and Religious Conquest of the Americas* (Louisville, KY: Westminster John Knox, 1992), 155.

[46] As quoted in Rivera, *A Violent Evangelism*, 155–156.

[47] Rivera, *A Violent Evangelism*, 156.

[48] Rivera, *A Violent Evangelism*, 156.

[49] Rivera, 156. On the destruction of indigenous images that were regarded as idolatrous by the Spanish colonizers, see Rivera, *A Violent Evangelism*, 160–168.

uneventful or as civil as they appear to have been in Cave 18 on Mona Island. Besides disparaging indigenous symbols as idols and burning indigenous texts, the Europeans used their own sacred texts to justify acts of great violence. Consider, for example, how Eduardo Galeano dramatizes the encounter that took place between the Inca leader Atahualpa and Francisco Pizarro at Cajamarca on November 16, 1532:

> A thousand men sweep the path of the Inca into the great square where the Spaniards wait in hiding. The multitude trembles at the passage of the Beloved Father, the One, the Only, lord of labors and fiestas; the singers fall silent, and the dancers freeze up. In the half light, last light of the day, the crowns and vestments of Atahualpa and his cortege of nobles of the realm gleam with gold and silver.
>
> Where are the gods brought by the wind? The Inca reaches the center of the square and gives the order to wait. A few days ago, a spy penetrated the camp of the invaders, tugged at their beards, and returned to report that they were no more than a handful of crooks from the sea. That blasphemy cost his life. Where are the sons of Wiwarocha, who wear stars on their heels and send forth thunders that provoke stupor, stampede, and death?
>
> The priest Vicente de Valverde emerges from the shadows and goes to meet Atahualpa. He raises the Bible in one hand and a crucifix in the other, as if exorcizing a storm on the high seas, and cries that here is God, the true one, and that all the rest is nonsense. The interpreter translates and Atahualpa, at the head of the throng, asks, "Who told you that?" "The Bible says it, the sacred book." "Give it here so it can tell me." A few paces away, Pizarro unsheathes his sword. Atahualpa looks at the Bible, turns

it over in his hand, shakes it to make it talk, and presses it against his ear: "It says nothing. It's empty." And he drops it to the ground.

Pizarro has been awaiting this moment ever since the day he knelt before Emperor Charles V, described the empire big as Europe that he had discovered and proposed to conquer, and promised him the most splendid treasure in human history. . . . Pizarro yells and pounces. At the signal, the trap is sprung. From the ambush trumpets blare, arquebuses roar, and the cavalry charges the stunned and unarmed crowd.[50]

Atahualpa's nephew Titu Cusi Yupanqui offers a somewhat different—though no less dramatic—account of the encounter between his uncle and Pizarro. According to him,

Two of these Virachochas were brought to my uncle Atahuallpa by some men from the Yunca people. At the time, Atahuallpa was staying at Cajamarca, where he received them very well. However, when he offered our customary drink in a golden cup to one of them, the Spaniard poured it out with his own hands, which offended my uncle very much. After that, those two Spaniards showed my uncle a letter or a book (I am not sure exactly which), explaining to him that this was the *quillca* [word] of God and of the king. My uncle, still offended by the wasting of the *chicha* (which is how we call our drink), took the letter (or whatever it was) and threw it down, saying, "What is this supposed to be that you gave to me here? Be gone!" Thereupon the Spaniards returned to their

---

[50] Eduardo Galeano, *Genesis: Memory of Fire Book 1*, trans. Cedric Belfrage (New York: Pantheon, 1987), 87–88.

companions and related to them what they had seen and what had happened during their dealings with my uncle Atahuallpa.[51]

The account explains the reasons for which the strangers were called *Viracochas*:

> This is the name that we used to apply to the creator of all things. . . . They named the people as such because they differed much from us in clothing and appearance and because they rode very large animals with silver feet (by which they meant the glittering horseshoes). Another reason for calling them so was that the Indians saw them alone talking to white cloths [paños blancos] as a person would speak to another, which is how the Indians perceived the reading of books and letters.[52]

According to this Inca account, it was only "many days later" that the massacre at Cajamarca took place. On learning that forty or fifty Spaniards had arrived in Cajamarca, Atahualpa made his way to meet them there, bringing no weapons for battle. Then,

> After having heard what they had to say, my uncle attended to them and calmly offered one of them a drink in the manner I have already described above in order to see if these people, too, would waste the drink as the other two had done before. And, indeed, it happened just like before; they neither drank it nor concerned themselves with it. Having seen how little they minded his things, my

---

[51] Titu Cusi Yupanqui, *An Inca Account of the Conquest of Peru*, translated, introduced, and annotated by Ralph Bauer (Boulder: University Press of Colorado, 2005), 60.

[52] Titu Cusi Yupanqui, *An Inca Account of the Conquest of Peru*, 60.

uncle said, "If you disrespect me, I will also disrespect you."
He got up angrily and raised a cry as though he wanted
to kill the Spaniards. However, the Spaniards were on the
lookout and took possession of the four gates of the plaza
where they were, which was enclosed on all its sides.[53]

Then the slaughter began. When it was over, "Of more than
ten thousand not even two hundred escaped," and Atahualpa was
taken prisoner and jailed, "stark naked and his neck in shackles."[54]

There are several somewhat differing versions of the fateful
encounter between Atahualpa and Pizarro at Cajamarca. In the introduction to his translation of Titu Cusi Yupanqui's, *An Inca Account of
the Conquest of Peru*, Ralph Bauer explains how Juan de Betanzos, the
Spaniard who was married to Atahualpa's sister recounted it:

> After the interpreter had explained to Atahuallpa that he
> should "obey the captain [Pizarro] who was also the son
> of the Sun, and that was what . . . the painting in the book
> said," Atahuallpa "asked for the book and, taking it in his
> hands he opened it. When he saw the lines of letters, he
> said, 'This speaks and says that you are the son of the Sun?
> I, also, am the son of the Sun.' . . . Saying this, he hurled the
> book away."[55]

Galeano's dramatization draws from the account of the event
provided in the seventeenth-century Guaman Poma de Ayala's
Nueva corónica y buen gobierno. As Bauer presents what the
contemporary sources reported, the Spanish attack

---

[53] Titu Cusi Yupanqui, *An Inca Account of the Conquest of Peru*,
61–62.

[54] Titu Cusi Yupanqui, *An Inca Account of the Conquest of Peru*, 62.

[55] Bauer, "Introduction," in *An Inca Account of the Conquest of Peru*,
loc. 351 of 2962.

was triggered when Atahuallpa, in a haughty gesture, flung the breviary presented to him by the priest Vicente de Valverde into the dust. The book contained the famous *requirimento* [*sic*] (Requirement), a text that by law had to be read aloud to the Natives and which informed them of their obligation to "acknowledge the Church and the Rule and Superior of the whole world . . . and the high priest called Pope, and in his name the King and the Queen." Noncompliance was legitimate ground for the commencement of violent conquest.[56]

In their review of the several different accounts of what transpired at Cajamarca, Diana Taylor and Sarah J. Townsend conclude, "Regardless of the facts, the book seems central to most versions of the actual event—though the irony is that Francisco Pizarro, the conqueror, could not read or write."[57] In the light of the massacre at Cajamarca, it comes as no surprise that in 1985, indigenous peoples of the Andes addressed the following words to Pope John Paul II:

We, the Indians of the Andes and the Americas have decided to give you back your Bible, since for the past five hundred years it has brought us neither love, peace, or justice. We beg you to take your Bible and give it to our oppressors, whose hearts and minds are in greater need of its moral teachings. As part of the colonial exchange we received the Bible, which is an ideological weapon of attack. The Spanish sword used in the daytime to attack and kill the Indians, turned at night into a cross which attacked the Indian soul.[58]

---

[56] Bauer, "Introduction," in *An Inca Account of the Conquest of Peru*, loc. 345 of 2962.

[57] Diana Taylor and Sarah J. Townsend, eds., *Stages of Conflict: A Critical Anthology of Latin American Theater and Performance* (Ann Arbor: University of Michigan Press, 2008), 60.

[58] See "Pope Asked to Take Back Bible," *The Telegraph*, February 7,

This is the background—with the book at its center— and its long memory of pain in contrast with which the *encuentro* in Cave 18 constitutes such a striking exception.

Turning back to the consideration of what happened on Mona Island during the sixteenth century, Cooper and his co-authors cautiously conclude that "the interaction between Christian commentary and indigenous imagery [*in Cave 18*] represents individual responses and a degree of mutual understanding, rather than a coherent programme or formal liturgy."[59] This, they suggest, was not typical of the colonial *encuentro*: "The emotional and theological character of the inscriptions is different from the censure of the inquisition in places such as contemporary Mexico, where the incorporation of indigenous iconography into a Calvary scene," as occurs in the inscription of two crosses on either side of an already existing indigenous anthropomorphic pictograph, "would have been deeply heretical."[60] The Mona researchers also hypothesize that "from an indigenous perspective, the lack of clear evidence for resistance, such as the depictions of cross-bearing Spanish horsemen from indigenous rock art in the Andes, and the lack of explicit continuity of traditional visual codes, points to a degree of ownership of new beliefs and practices."[61] If even some of the crosses in Cave 18 can be demonstrated to have been the work of Taíno Christians, that would provide support for the claim that at least some of the indigenous population of Mona embraced the beliefs of their Spanish colonizers.

Cooper and his co-authors accurately point out how "the historical legacy of 1492 fixates upon and fetishises the incompatibility of native and European worldviews, leading to a one-sided

1985; also Pablo Richard, "1492: The Violence of God and the Future of Christianity," *Concilium* 6 (1990): 66.

[59] Cooper et al., "'The Mona Chronicle,'" 1067.
[60] Cooper et al., "'The Mona Chronicle,'" 1067.
[61] Cooper et al., "'The Mona Chronicle,'" 1067.

picture of the spiritual conquest of the Americas, exacerbated by native 'extinction' in the Caribbean. Moreover, the sheer continental scale of colonisation means that grand narratives dominate our image of encounter."[62] In contrast to such grand narrative, though, what happened when two worldviews met in Cave 18 was an encounter of a different order of magnitude. As Cooper and his co-authors note, "The individual narrative of the people who actually made these encounters operates at a temporal resolution of minutes, hours and days as revealed within this cave."[63]

Cooper and his colleagues conclude "The Mona Chronicle" by calling attention to a most curious coincidence:

> In 1550, King Charles V of Spain presided over a theological debate in Valladolid (Las Casas–Sepúlveda debate) about whether the Indians of the New World had rational souls. In the same year, Alonso Pérez Roldan the Younger and Myguel Rypoll partook in a procession to a local shrine, etched their names onto the walls of a cave chamber and joined a debate in this cave about the compatibility of the Catholic God and ancestral spirits with the *indios* who led them there.[64]

The difference between these two events and their settings was far more than a matter of the many miles of ocean that separated them. Even so, "both express the metaphysical schisms, anxieties, social experiments and transformations engendered on all sides

---

[62] Cooper et al., "'The Mona Chronicle,'" 1067.

[63] Cooper et al., "'The Mona Chronicle,'" 1067.

[64] Cooper et al., "'The Mona Chronicle,'" 1068. See the well-known treatment of the Valladolid disputation by Lewis Hanke, *All Mankind Is One: A Study of the Disputation between Bartolomé de Las Casas and Juan Ginés de Sepúlveda in 1550 on the Intellectual and Religious Capacity of the American Indians* (DeKalb: Northern Illinois University Press, 1974).

by the European-American encounters."[65] What they share in common is more important by far than what distinguishes them. The distance between Valladolid and what transpired there in 1550 and Mona Island and what happened there in the years around 1550 is dramatically remapped when we seriously consider the implications of the *encuentro* that took place in Cave 18.

Media and Message

Has too much been made of this *encuentro* that took place in the middle of the sixteenth century deep in the dark confines of a cave located on a small island that is almost equally distant from the coast of the Dominican Republic to the west and Puerto Rico to the east? What does it mean when a discovery like this about something that took place more than five centuries ago—and not only the news of stranded refugees coming ashore there in our own times—brings Mona Island to the attention of *National Geographic* and *Smithsonian*, as well as Fox News?

I would argue that what happened in Cave 18 in the middle of the sixteenth century is just as momentous as the debate that took place an ocean away in Valladolid if we take *lo cotidiano*—lived daily experience—seriously as a vital *locus theologicus*. In effect, what archaeologists have helped us retrieve by their investigation of Cave 18 is a centuries-old moment in the daily lives of the indigenous inhabitants of Mona Island and the Spanish colonizers who had found their way to the chambers where their worldviews encountered each other and quite literally left their marks behind. Thus it is not only at the high level academic debates in Valladolid that the relationship between colonizers and colonized was mapped from above, but also in the hand-drawn marks with which both Taínos and Spaniards mapped their relationships—

---

[65] Cooper et al., "'The Mona Chronicle,'" 1068.

quite literally—from below. In effect, the sophisticated and careful work done by the researchers of the *Corazón del Caribe* project involved retrieval of the material traces of the lived daily experience of the sixteenth-century inhabitants of Mona, Taínos and Europeans alike.

As Carmen Nanko-Fernández has written, Latin@s affirm that lived daily reality is a source for divine revelation and as such it is worthy of theological reflection. Furthermore, "Lo cotidiano provides the *content* for theologizing. The concrete and miscellaneous stuff of life informs humble attempts to articulate understandings of the sacred and their implications for our relationships with each other and the whole of creation."[66] Popular religion is among the "slices" of lived daily experience to which Nanko-Fernández calls attention. She explains that, according to Orlando Espín, "the faith of the people presented 'an epistemology—a way of knowing and constructing the "real" by means that are culturally specific.'"[67] For Nanko-Fernández, the "texts" of *lo cotidiano*, "in all of their complexity, are embedded and embodied theological reflections that evoke and reflect creative, affective, sensuous, and even kinetic means of responding to the divine presence in the concrete circumstances and quotidian rhythms of human experience."[68]

Latin@ theologians have more often than not focused on

---

[66] Carmen Nanko-Fernández, "Lo Cotidiano as Locus Theologicus," in *The Wiley Blackwell Companion to Latino/a Theology*, ed. Orlando O. Espín (Oxford, UK: Wiley-Blackwell, 2015), 16.

[67] Nanko-Fernández, "Lo Cotidiano as Locus Theologicus," quoting Orlando O. Espín, "Traditioning: Culture, Daily Life and Popular Religion, and Their Impact on Christian Theology," in *Futuring Our Past: Explorations in the Theology of Tradition*, ed. Orlando O. Espín and Gary Macy (Maryknoll, NY: Orbis Books, 2006), 9.

[68] Carmen Nanko-Fernández, "Performative Theologies: Ritualizing the Daily Latinamente (2014)," updated and reprinted in *The Wiley Blackwell Reader in Practical Theology*, ed. Bonnie Miller McLemore (Oxford, UK: Wiley Blackwell, 2019), 81.

the practices of Christian popular religion in their attention to lived daily experience. A retrieval of the *encuentro* in Cave 18 of Mona Island offers us an opportunity to consider the evidence of indigenous popular religion and the ways in which Europeans first responded to the rock art. In charting a theology of revelation that takes Cave 18 into account, this exploration of *lo cotidiano*, as it found expression there, lingers with interest over the remark of Bartolomé de las Casas that Luis Rivera finds "theologically interesting," namely, that the indigenous peoples of the Americas "had a special knowledge of the true God." While las Casas may not have elaborated on how they came to such "special knowledge," the two Latin inscriptions found in Cave 18 suggest that the Spanish visitors who inscribed them had ideas of their own about the breadth of divine self-disclosure, ideas that may not have been shared by the visitor who was responsible for the Spanish-language inscription. Embracing Espín's affirmation that the faith of the people offers culturally specific ways (plural) of knowing and constructing the real, we need to interrogate the culturally specific ways that the faith of the sixteenth-century Spanish visitors to Mona Cave 18 made it possible for them to write "*Plura fecit Deus*" and "*Verbum caro factum est*," and also for another of their contemporaries to write "*Dios te perdone*."

In the following chapter, this quest will take us from Mona Island back across the Atlantic Ocean to sixteenth-century Spain and even to Valladolid, though not to the 1550 disputation that took place there between Bartolomé de las Casas and Juan Ginés de Sepúlveda. There we hope to discover the conditions that led to the articulation of a hermeneutics of the vernacular that helps to make sense of the Latin inscriptions of Cave 18. Let me be clear: I will not be arguing that a straight line can be drawn between what transpired in Cave 18 and what was percolating in Spain. The much more modest aim of what follows is to consider some ways in which the culturally specific currents in sixteenth-century Spanish thinking—specifically about the translation of Scripture—can help to frame the theological vision according to which the European visitors to Mona Island's Cave 18 came to terms with the Taíno images they found there.

CHAPTER 2

VERBUM CARO FACTUM EST

The Vernacular and the Incarnation

Chapter one left us with questions that call for further exploration, not only the kinds of questions that archaeologists will help us to address as they continue to explore Mona Island and its many caves, but also hermeneutical and theological questions. Little is known about the identity of who inscribed "*Dios te perdone*," "*Plura fecit Deus*," and "*Verbum caro factum est*" deep inside Cave 18, except for the first name—Bernardo—of the visitor who was probably responsible for that third inscription, and the likely dating of these inscriptions to the middle of the sixteenth century. While these inscriptions and other paleographic evidence led archaeologists to conclude that the sixteenth-century visitors to the cave were likely of Iberian origin, and that royal and ecclesiastical officials were among them, we know nothing specific enough about their backgrounds or about their education to know with any certainty what they were thinking during their *encuentros* with the Taínos and their glyphs.[1] Neither do we have the luxury of knowing

---

[1] See Alice V. M. Samson, Jago Cooper, and Josué Caamaño-Dones, "European Visitors to Native Spaces: Using Paleography to Investigate Early Religious Dynamics in the New World," *Latin American Antiquity* 27, no. 4 (2016): esp. 458, suggesting a series of visits by Europeans to this cave "minimally between August 1550 and February 1554."

what books they may or may not have brought along with them on their westward voyage to the Americas. What we might be able to retrieve, though, is some sense of what was in the air in sixteenth-century Spain that could have prompted them both to leave the indigenous symbols intact and to comment as they did. The archaeologists who explored Cave 18 pointed to the debate between Bartolomé de las Casas and Juan Ginés de Sepúlveda at Valladolid in 1550–1551 to set the *encuentro* between Spanish colonists and indigenous Taínos on Mona Island in a broader context. Cooper and his colleagues conclude that "the contrast between the formal, intellectual, metropolitan debate, immortalised in paper archives, and the dialogue between colonial individuals of diverse origins, materialised in stone, could not be greater."[2] While the Valladolid debate leaves no doubt that experiences in the American colonies had a substantial impact on theological discussions in Spain, it makes equally good sense to recognize that the visitors to Cave 18 responded in language that reflects intellectual currents that were circulating in Spain during the sixteenth century.

That is hardly specific enough to be helpful, especially when we pause to mention some of the events that took place in 1492, the year that many have identified—albeit unofficially—as the beginning of the *Siglo de Oro*, the "Golden Age" of Spanish arts and letters that actually lasted until 1659.[3] On April 17, 1492, Ferdinand II of Aragon and Isabella of Castile granted Christopher Columbus the

---

[2] Jago Cooper, Alice V. M. Samson, Miguel A. Nieves, Michael J. Lace, Josué Caamaño-Dones, Caroline Cartwright, Patricia N. Kambesis, and Laura del Olmo Frese, "'The Mona Chronicle': The Archaeology of Early Religious Encounter in the New World," *Antiquity* 90, no. 352 (2016): 1068. Also See Jean-Pierre Ruiz, "Cardinal Francisco Ximénes de Cisneros and Bartolomé de Las Casas, the 'Procurator and Universal Protector of all the Indians in the Indies,'" *Journal of Hispanic / Latino Theology* 9 (February 2002): 60–77.

[3] For a convenient overview, see Miguel Zorita Bayón, *Breve Historia del Siglo de Oro* (Madrid: Ediciones Nowtilus, 2011).

charter known as the *Capitulaciones de Santa Fe*, so named because it was drafted at Santa Fe de la Vega, in the camp from which the campaign proceeded against the Nasrid emirate of Granada, the final move of the *Reconquista*.[4] It was in March of 1492 that the Alhambra Decree was promulgated by Ferdinand and Isabella, mandating the expulsion from Spain of all Jews who refused to be baptized as Christians. The enforcement of that decree began on July 31, 1492, just three days before Columbus set sail on his first voyage.[5]

Columbus brought with him an interpreter named Luis de Torres, about whom the Diary of that first voyage says that he "had been a Jew and knew Hebrew and Chaldean and also some Arabic."[6] It was in August of 1492, while Columbus and his ships and their crews were under way westward, that Antonio de Nebrija published his *Arte de la lengua castellana*, the first such treatment of a European vernacular language to appear in print, modeled after the Latin grammar he had written a few years earlier.[7] When Queen Isabella was presented with the first

---

[4] See Joseph F. O'Callaghan, *The Last Crusade in the West: Castile and the Conquest of Granada* (Philadelphia: University of Pennsylvania Press, 2014). Also see Brian A. Catlos, *Kingdoms of Faith: A New History of Islamic Spain* (New York: Basic Books, 2018).

[5] See Norman Roth, *Conversos, Inquisition, and the Expulsion of the Jews from Spain* (Madison: University of Wisconsin Press, 2002). Also see Jean-Pierre Ruiz, *Readings from the Edges: The Bible & People on the Move* (Maryknoll, NY: Orbis Books, 2011), 132–133.

[6] "Avía sido judío y sabía dizque ebrayco y caldeo y aun algo arávigo" (Christopher Columbus, "Diario of 1492," Early Modern Spain, Research at King's College London, http://www.ems.kcl.ac.uk/content/etext/e019. html#d0e561). Also available in Oliver Dunn and James E. Kelley Jr., *The Diario of Christopher Columbus's First Voyage to America, 1492–1493* (Norman: University of Oklahoma Press, 1989), 128–129.

[7] As Carlos G. Noreña writes, "The indisputable champion of the vernacular during the reign of the Catholic Kings was Antonio de Nebrija, whose *Arte de la lengua Castellana* . . . was the first grammar of the vernacular ever published in Europe. Nebrija's central idea was that

copy of Nebrija's new grammar in a ceremony at the University of
Salamanca, Hernando de Talavera, the bishop of Ávila, explained,
"After your Highness has subjected barbarous peoples and nations
of varied tongues . . . with conquest will come the need for them
to accept the laws that the conqueror imposes on the conquered,
and among them will be our language."[8] Henry Kamen explains
how Nebrija himself wrote in the preface to his grammar, "I
have found one conclusion to be very true, that language always
accompanies empire, both have always commenced, grown, and
flourished together."[9]

Even the briefest glimpse of what transpired in 1492 helps
to chart the complexity of the Iberian political, cultural, literary,
and religious landscape that shaped the consciousness—and the
consciences—of those who sailed westward with Columbus and

Castilian had reached its full maturity to become the language of an
emerging empire and in no respect was it inferior to Latin (*Studies in
Spanish Renaissance Thought* [The Hague: Martinus Nijhoff, 1975], 187).

[8] Quoted in Henry Kamen, *Empire: How Spain Became a World
Power, 1492–1763* (New York: Harper Collins, 2004), 3.

[9] Kamen, *Empire: How Spain Became a World Power*, 3. Kamen writes
that "while Castilians enjoyed almost unlimited political horizons, they
contracted their cultural perspectives by defining in a wholly exclusive
sense what it meant to be a 'Spaniard.' Unlike the Roman Empire before
them and the British Empire after them, they attempted to exclude from
their midst all alternative cultures, beginning with two of the great historic
cultures of the peninsula. From the year 1492, which marked the capitu-
lation of Granada and the expulsion of the Jews, both Islam and Judaism
were effectively excluded from the Spanish concept of the universe"
(*Empire: How Spain Became a World Power*, 342). As for the rapid growth
of Castilian as the national language of a unified Spain, Noreña offers the
example of the Holy Roman Emperor and King of Spain Charles V (1500–
1555) himself: "At the age of eighteen Charles V did not know a word of
Castilian; at age twenty-four his speech was a bizarre mixture of French and
Spanish; at thirty-six, however, he had the audacity to address Pope Paul III
in Spanish, 'such a noble language—' he said 'that deserves to be known by
every Christian'" (*Studies in Spanish Renaissance Thought*, 188).

those who followed afterwards, including perhaps even those who found their way to Mona Island beginning in 1493. Given the importance of language, and of the Castilian vernacular in particular, what might we learn from considering the sixteenth-century authors whose works might be found on a bookshelf in Salamanca or in Valladolid ? Of course, we would find the writings of literary luminaries including Miguel de Cervantes and Lope de Vega, Luis de Góngora and Garcilaso de la Vega, among others. Influential theologians of that era we would include Melchor Cano, Domingo de Soto, and Francisco de Vitoria, and among the mystics the likes of the great Carmelite reformers Juan de la Cruz and Teresa de Ávila.[10] We might also find the Bible translated into Spanish by Casiodoro de Reina (published in 1569) and subsequently revised (in 1602) by Cipriano de Valera, even though these two were forced to flee Spain as heretics.[11]

As influential as these authors all were, I will focus instead on the Augustinian Fray Luis de León (1527–1591), professor at the University of Salamanca and prisoner of the Inquisition, theologian, commentator on the Bible, translator of the Song of Songs and the book of Job as well as works by Virgil, Horace, Pindar, and Euripides. Fray Luis was a gifted poet in his own right, although his own original poems—now much studied and applauded as lyrical masterpieces of the *Siglo de Oro*—remained unpublished during his own lifetime.[12] Miguel de Cervantes wrote of Fray Luis,

---

[10] On Juan de la Cruz, see the work of Miguel H. Díaz in this Disruptive Cartographers series, *Queer God de Amor* (New York, NY: Fordham University Press, 2022).

[11] See A. Gordon Kinder, *Casiodoro de Reina: Spanish Reformer of the Sixteenth Century* (London: Tamesis, 1975); Raymond S. Rosales, *Casiodoro de Reina: Patriarca del Protestantismo Hispano* (St. Louis, MO: Concordia Seminary, 2002).

[12] See Fray Luis de León, *Obras Completas Castellanas II. Exposición del libro de Job, Poesías*, 5th ed. (Madrid: Biblioteca de Autores Cristianos, 1991), 742–799. Carlos G. Noreña writes that "In spite of Fray Luis'

"I would like to end my song . . . with the praise for the genius who astounds the world and in his ecstasy might rob us of our senses. All that I have shown till now appears in the figure of Fray Luis de León, whom I revere, adore, and follow."[13] Together with all that, it is Fray Luis who was responsible for editing the first published edition (1588) of the writings of Teresa de Ávila.[14] Despite the considerable—and well-deserved—attention and acclaim that Fray Luis has received from historians, philosophers, biblical scholars, theologians and scholars of literature in Spanish, not nearly as much has been written about him in English.[15]

---

merits as a theologian and spiritual writer, his name and reputation have been almost exclusively linked with his achievements as a poet" (*Studies in Spanish Renaissance Thought* [The Hague: Martinus Nijhoff, 1975], 170). Fray Luis wrote, "I never knew nor saw Mother Teresa de Jesús while she was on earth, but now that she lives in Heaven I know and see her almost constantly in two vivid images which she has left of herself, and these are her spiritual daughters and her books. Which in my judgment are also faithful witnesses . . . they bear witness to her great virtue" (as quoted in Luis de León, *The Names of Christ*, translation and introduction by Manuel Durán and William Kluback (Ramsey, NJ: Paulist Press, 1984), 23.

[13] As quoted in Bernard McGinn, *Mysticism in the Golden Age of Spain 1500–1650* (New York: Crossroad, 2017), 338–339.

[14] See Geneviève Fabry, "El Cantar de los Cantares en la obra de Luis de León, San Juan de la Cruz y Juan Gelman: Lengua, infancia y experiencia spiritual," *Jornadas Diálogos: Literatura, Estética y Teología. La libertad del Espíritu, V*, September 17–19, 2013 (Buenos Aires: Universidad Católica Argentina, Facultad de Filosofía y Letras, 2013), https://repositorio.uca.edu.ar/bitstream/123456789/4868/1/cantar-cantares-luis-leon.pdf. I am grateful to Miguel H. Díaz for bringing this article to my attention.

[15] *The Names of Christ*, published in the Paulist Press Classics of Western Spirituality series in 1984, is the most widely known of his works (Luis de León, *The Names of Christ*, translation and introduction by Manuel Durán and William Kluback). This is the first complete translation of *The Names of Christ* into English. See the review by Colin P. Thompson in *New Blackfriars* 66 (1985); 201–202. Among the relatively few English translations of works by Fray Luis that are available, see Fray Luis de León,

What I offer here is not a comprehensive consideration of Fray Luis or of his extensive and varied body of work. That would be too ambitious, nor would it serve the specific purpose that this limited and closely focused retrieval seeks to accomplish. I want to suggest that the advocacy for the vernacular that was energetically advanced by Fray Luis and that he deliberately practiced in his own translations (especially of texts from the Bible) into Spanish and in his own original Spanish language works (including *The Names of Christ*) is closely bound up with his appreciation of the significance of the Incarnation of the Word. This makes it possible to recognize in the work of Fray Luis the beginnings of a theology of vernacular language that provided a solid rationale for the translation of the Bible into Spanish amid the controversies of the sixteenth century. It also indirectly but very suggestively offers an appropriate and contemporary framework for considering the implicit theologies that underlie the European inscriptions in Cave 18 on Mona Island. Before moving in that direction, it is worth considering what Fray Luis himself may have known about the indigenous peoples of the Americas and what his views were vis-à-vis the Spanish colonial project.

Fray Luis and the Americas

What Fray Luis Read about the Americas

How did Fray Luis, who never left Spain, become aware of the "New World" and its peoples? Fortunately, there is no need to resort to mere speculation about what he may have heard either

---

A Bilingual Edition of Fray Luis de León's La Perfecta Casada: The Role of Married Women in Sixteenth-Century Spain, ed. and trans. John A. Jones and Javier San José Lera (Lewiston, NY: Edwin Mellen Press, 1999). Also see Fray Luis de León, *The Unknown Light: The Poems of Fray Luis de León*, trans. Willis Barnstone (Albany: State University of New York Press, 1979).

directly or indirectly, because we have documentation of his work as an official censor of José de Acosta's *Historia natural y moral de las Indias*, the extensive and wide-ranging treatment that includes geography, climate, flora and fauna, indigenous history, customs, and practices by this Jesuit missionary to Peru and Mexico. Fray Luis wrote:

> I have seen this *Natural and Moral History of the Indies* written by Father José de Acosta of the Society of Jesus, and it is Catholic in matters pertaining to the doctrine of the Faith, and as for the rest worthy of the great learning and prudence of the author and worthy of causing all who read it to praise God, who is so wonderful in all his works. Given in San Felipe de Madrid on May 4, 1589.[16]

A footnote explains that "in the sixteenth century, the Inquisition regularly submitted texts to a university committee for review," and it is Fray Luis who was charged with providing the *nihil obstat* for Acosta's book, the certification that nothing in the work was at odds with Catholic teaching. "Even though he had never been to the Americas," the note tells us, "León read and approved Acosta's chronicle of New World history in his capacity as a chaired

---

[16] José de Acosta, *Natural and Moral History of the Indies*, ed. Jane E. Mangan, with an introduction and commentary by Walter D. Mignolo, translated by Frances Lopez-Morillas (Durham, NC: Duke University Press, 2002), 4. "He visto esta Historia Natural y Moral de las Indias, que escriue el Padre Ioseph de Acosta de la Compañia de Iesus, y en lo que toca a la doctrina de la Fee, es Catolica, y en lo demas Digna de las muchas letras y prudencia del Autor, y de que todos la lean, para que alaben a Dios, que tan marauilloso es en sus obras. En San Felipe de Madrid a quatro de Mayo de 1589." (Spanish text from https://archive.org/details/historianaturaly-00acos/page/n9/mode/2up.) On José de Acosta, see Claudio M. Burgaleta, *José de Acosta, S.J. (1540–1600): His Life and Thought* (Chicago: Loyola University Press, 2003).

professor of sacred scripture at the University of Salamanca."[17] Acosta's book received particular scrutiny because it was written "during an era of hypersensitivity to the study of indigenous history because in 1577 King Philip II had ordered the censorship of all publications on native customs and rituals."[18]

Taking a look at the statement itself, Fray Luis begins by reporting his finding that, with respect to matters of faith, the book is in conformity with Catholic doctrine. It is worth noting that this is a limited judgment that focuses specifically on those portions of the book that have to do with "the doctrine of the Faith." Strictly speaking, such a *nihil obstat* does not constitute an endorsement on the part of the censor, but only an affirmation that no doctrinal error stands in the way of the work's publication.[19] Fray Luis applauds the rest of the book, albeit succinctly, commending Acosta and affirming that his work is "worthy of causing all who read it to praise God, who is so wonderful in all his works." Before looking more closely at what Fray Luis learned from reading Acosta's book, it is worth pausing to note the remarkable similarity between the compliment offered by the Augustinian academic and one of the two Latin inscriptions in Cave 18. Fray Luis declares

---

[17] José de Acosta, *Natural and Moral History of the Indies*, 4, note 1.

[18] José de Acosta, *Natural and Moral History of the Indies*, 4, note 1. Doris Heyden writes: "A *cédula* of April 22, 1577, sent by Philip II to Viceroy Martín Enríquez, prohibited all writings referring to 'superstitions and the ways of life of the Indians' in any language and specifically ordered the confiscation of the extensive works of [*Bernardino de*] Sahagún, as well as of other writings of similar character. Many major chronicles were effectively repressed, some of them unknown until their rediscovery in the nineteenth century (in Fray Diego Durán, *The History of the Indies of New Spain*, trans. and ed. Doris Heyden [Norman: University of Oklahoma Press, 1994], xxxii).

[19] Besides the *nihil obstat* by Fray Luis, Acosta's book also includes an *imprimi potest*, a permission to publish, from King Philip II and another by the Jesuit provincial superior Gonzalo Dávila.

the book "worthy of causing all who read it to praise God, who is so wonderful in all his works," and the anonymous Iberian visitor recorded his own words of praise, "Plura fecit Deus." To read Acosta's book, Fray Luis affirmed, is to be inspired to marvel at the wonders of God's many works in the Americas, a sentiment that is fully consonant with *"plura fecit Deus."*[20]

Given the broad range of topics treated in Acosta's *Historia natural y moral de las Indias*, we have no way of knowing whether or not Fray Luis was pleased with what Acosta had to say about volcanoes in book three, or about his explanation of yucca, cassava, potatoes, and plantains in book four, or about the Jesuit's description and assessment of indigenous religious practices in book five. In his valuable study of Acosta, Claudio Burgaleta—himself a Jesuit—explains that while some authors understand the structure of Acosta's *Historia* "as following Aristotle's hierarchy or ladder of being, moving from a consideration of inanimate creation through the vegetative and animal kingdoms to the zenith of creation, the world of culture created by rational creatures."[21] There is more at work here theologically, Burgaleta suggests. This has to do with the Jesuit spirituality that inspired Acosta, who entered the recently established Society of Jesus (at the age of thirteen) in 1553, just fourteen years after Pope Paul III granted approval to the Society in 1540.[22] According to Burgaleta, the structure of Acosta's *Historia* reflects the influence of the Spiritual Exercises of Ignatius of Loyola, more specifically the contemplation to attain love

---

[20] Is it possible that Fray Luis had Psalm 145 (Vulgate 144) in mind as he composed this *nihil obstat*? "Magnus Dominus, et laudabilis nimis, et magnitudinis ejus non est finis. . . . Fidelis Dominus in omnibus verbis suis, et sanctus in omnibus operibus suis." / "The Lord is great and most worthy of praise, and his greatness is without end. . . . The Lord is faithful in all his words, and holy in all his deeds" (English translation mine).

[21] Burgaleta, *José de Acosta*, 108.

[22] Burgaleta, *José de Acosta*, 108.

(*contemplatio ad amorem*) in the fourth week of the Exercises.[23] Burgaleta explains: "Ignatius wants the retreatant to contemplate how God is present in his creatures proceeding up the ladder of being from the elements or mineral realm, through the world of plants, on to the realm of animals, and culminating in the world of humans."[24] Burgaleta argues convincingly that his sixteenth-century Jesuit confrere "imitates this structure of the *contemplatio ad amorem* by structuring the *Historia* as an ascent up the ladder of being in which he highlights the new marvels of God's creation in the Americas," and that for him, "the greatest of these wonders was the work of redemption of the native peoples that he believed God was working in the Indies even as he was writing."[25]

It is ultimately unnecessary to choose between Aristotle and Ignatius in a debate over which of them influenced the structure of the *Historia*, because the theological perspective that is the fruit of Acosta's familiarity with the Spiritual Exercises only adds to the significance of how his is arranged. After all, the "ladder of being" involved in the *contemplatio ad amorem* reflects an underlying Aristotelian perspective that would have been a common feature in European thinking and that was certainly familiar to Acosta.[26] As Burgaleta writes, Acosta's narrative is "an invaluable chronicle of the zoological, botanical, meteorological, geophysical, ethnological, anthropological, and sociological marvels he encountered in the Indies."[27] Yet, in the

---

[23] See George Ganss, *The Spiritual Exercises of Saint Ignatius, A Translation and Commentary* (Chicago: Loyola Press, 1992), nos. 230–237.

[24] Burgaleta, *José de Acosta*, 107.

[25] Burgaleta, *José de Acosta*, 108.

[26] The *Historia* makes a number of explicit references to Aristotle, among them chapter nine of book one, "Of Aristotle's opinion of the New World and what it was that caused him to deny it" (Acosta, *Natural and Moral History*, 34–37).

[27] Burgaleta, *José de Acosta*, 109.

light of the Ignatian *Exercises*, as "a contemplative in action, Acosta finds God no less in the natural marvels of the Americas than in what at first glance may be the demonic religion of the native peoples."[28] Burgaleta demonstrates that "Acosta's skill in finding God in all things," which is a key dimension of Ignatian spirituality, "allows him to argue in the *Historia* that the demonic practices of the native peoples were a marvelous example of Providence that brought good out of evil."[29]

On the surface of it, this might seem odd. After all, book five of Acosta's *Historia* begins with a chapter on "How the Devil's pride and envy have been the cause of idolatry," and the following chapter offers a classification of "the kinds of idolatries used by the Indians."[30] In book five Acosta also discusses (in chapter eleven) "How the devil has tried to copy God in methods of sacrifices and of religion and sacraments," finding what he believed to be evidence of such activity in the Americas.[31] This includes temples (chapter twelve), among them "splendid temples" in Mexico (chapter thirteen), priests and the offices they performed (chapter fourteen), "monasteries of virgins that the devil invented for his service" (chapter fifteen), and "monasteries of religious that the devil possesses for his superstition" (chapter sixteen). Acosta's descriptions in book five of the *Historia* of what he regarded as demonic simulation of Christian practices also include "How the devil has tried to mimic the sacraments of Holy Church" (chapter twenty-three), "How the devil tried in Mexico to mimic the feast of Corpus Christi and the communion used by Holy Church" (chapter twenty-four), "Of the confession and confessors used by the Indians" (chapter twenty-five), and "Of some festivals that the

---

[28] Burgaleta, *José de Acosta*, 109.

[29] Burgaleta, "*José de Acosta*," 109.

[30] Acosta, *Natural and Moral History*, 253–254, 256–257.

[31] Acosta, *Natural and Moral History*, 275.

Indians of Cuzco had and how the devil also tried to imitate the mystery of the Holy Trinity" (chapter twenty-eight).

By claiming that indigenous religious practices represented demonically inspired mirror images of Christian practices and doctrines, Acosta was "demonstrating that Providence was able to prepare the way for efficacious preaching of the gospel by using the idolatrous rituals of the Amerindians to prefigure the sacraments of the Roman Catholic Church." So, in Acosta's view, "in their own way even these base pagan belief and practices helped people to find God."[32] According to Acosta, the devil's strategy of configuring indigenous "idolatry" actually provided Christian missionaries with a tactical advantage: the demonic mimicry he described constituted a sort of *praeparatio evangelica*. Framed in Ignatian terms as a matter of finding God in all things, it also represents a claim on Acosta's part that the Americas were contested territory where God and the devil were in direct competition with each other for the souls of indigenous people. In chapter one of book five, Acosta writes that "once idolatry was rooted out of the best and noblest part of the world, the devil retired to the most remote places and reigned in that part of the world, which, although it is very inferior in nobility, is not so in size and breadth."[33] While Acosta does not say so in as many words, it can be inferred that the extirpation of idolatry from "the best and noblest part of the world" is a reference to Spain, to the *Reconquista* of Spain from Muslim rule and to the Alhambra Decree and its impact on the Jews of Spain.[34]

Here too we find echoes of the *Spiritual Exercises*, the meditation on two standards—that of Christ and that of Lucifer—which is found on the fourth day of the second week. The retreatant is

---

[32] Burgaleta, *José de Acosta*, 108.

[33] Acosta, *Natural and Moral History*, 254.

[34] This is especially ironic in view of Acosta's own *converso* background. See John W. O'Malley, *The First Jesuits* (Cambridge, MA: Harvard University Press, 1993), 223–224.

invited to imagine two armies on a battlefield, one under the banner or standard of Christ and the other under the standard of Lucifer.[35] While in the *Exercises* this meditation focuses on the retreatant's individual discernment, in Acosta's *Historia* the battle between Christ and Lucifer was being played out as a contest in which the missionaries understood themselves under the standard of Christ. Questions about the rules of engagement in this battle, about appropriate tactics, and about what constituted acceptable collateral damage were the focus of intense debate.

Even as Acosta devoted many pages of his *Historia* to the idolatrous practices of the indigenous peoples of the Americas and the demonic inspiration underlying these practices, he interrupts his account of these idolatries in book six with chapter three, where he considers "how there is some knowledge of God among the Indians."[36] This chapter begins by admitting that "First, although the gross darkness of unbelief has obscured the minds of those nations, in many ways the light of truth and reason works in them to some small degree; and so most of them acknowledge and confess a supreme Lord and Maker of all."[37] This belief, Acosta notes, is not peculiar to Peruvians alone, because "the same belief exists, after their fashion, in the Mexicans and the Chinese today and in other heathen peoples."[38] It is unclear why Acosta extends the range of his observation to include not only the Americas but China as well.[39]

---

[35] See Ganss, *The Spiritual Exercises of Saint Ignatius*, nos. 136–147.

[36] Acosta, *Natural and Moral History*, 256.

[37] Acosta, *Natural and Moral History*, 256.

[38] Acosta, *Natural and Moral History*, 256.

[39] This is not the only place in the *Historia* where Acosta mentions China. In book six, for example, chapter five considers "the kinds of letters and books that the Chinese use," and chapter six speaks "of universities and studies in China." A footnote explains that "Acosta is unique in his efforts to draw the people of the East Indies into a comparison and classification with the Inca and the Aztecs," and he posits that Acosta's "information on

Acosta points to Acts 17:23 to frame what he has to say about the knowledge of God among the indigenous peoples of the Americas,

> This is very similar to what is told in the Book of Acts of the Apostles, when Saint Paul was in Athens and saw an altar with the inscription 'Ignoto Deo,' to the unknown God, from which the apostle took the subject of his preaching, telling them, "What therefore you worship without knowing it, that I preach to you."[40]

Just as the apostle Paul took advantage of the Athenians' veneration of "the unknown God" to proclaim the Gospel of Christ, Acosta explained that "all those who preach the Gospel to the Indians today have little difficulty in persuading them that there is a supreme God

China and Japan likely came from his association in Mexico and en route to Spain, with Fr. Alonso Sánchez, who was a missionary in the Philippines. At the time Acosta met him, Sánchez was traveling home to Spain to lobby for a military campaign against the Chinese, as his experience in the East Indies had convinced him that the evangelizing process would never progress without an accompanying military force" (José de Acosta, *Natural and Moral History*, 284, note 1). The same note explains that Sánchez was only one of a number of Jesuits who were active in Asia during the sixteenth century, and that Matteo Ricci is by far the better known of these missionaries. On Ricci, see R. Po-Chia Hsia, *A Jesuit in the Forbidden City: Matteo Ricci 1552–1610* (New York: Oxford University Press, 2010), as well as Michela Fontana, *Matteo Ricci: A Jesuit in the Ming Court* (Lanham, MD: Rowman & Littlefield, 2011). Acosta's interest in correlations between China and the Americas might also have to do with his suggestion in chapter twenty of book one that "it is more reasonable that the first dwellers of the Indies came by land" from Asia and not by sea. On the considerable complications that are involved in this, see Helga Gemegah, "Did the idea about the Asian origin of the American 'Indians' develop from 16th century Spanish political geography?" *Studies in Historical Anthropology*, vol. 2 (2005), 3–16.

[40] Acosta, *Natural and Moral History*, 256.

and Lord of all, and that he is the God of the Christians and the true God."[41] Thus, for Acosta the belief in a "supreme Lord and Maker of all" among indigenous Americans served to create conditions that were hospitable to Christian missionary activity.

Acosta then signals what he regards as something more than just a problem of translation, expressing astonishment that "even though they do have the knowledge that I mention, they have no word of their own with which to name God," finding no word in indigenous languages that corresponds to Dios or *Deus* or *Theos* or *El* or *Allah*.[42] For that reason, "those who preach or write for the Indians use our Spanish word *Dios*, adjusting its pronunciation and accent to the properties of the Indian languages, which are very diverse." In the judgment of Acosta, "This shows what a weak and incomplete knowledge they [*indigenous people of the Americas*] have of God, for they do not even know how to name him except by using our word."[43]

Even so, says Acosta, "indeed they did have a sort of knowledge" of God, as evidence of which he writes that "they built a very splendid temple to him in Peru, calling it Pachacamac, which was the chief sanctuary of the realm. And as I have said, *Pachacamac* means the same as *Creator*, although they also performed their idolatries in this temple, worshiping the devil and making representations of him."[44] This observation, based in part on the translation of *Pachacamac*, effectively mitigates Acosta's own argument about

---

[41] Acosta, *Natural and Moral History*, 256.

[42] Acosta, *Natural and Moral History*, 257.

[43] Acosta, *Natural and Moral History*, 257. A footnote points out that this implies indigenous languages were ineffective for missionary activity, but that "Other participants in the sixteenth century debate on native languages, such as the Dominican Santo Tomás, who authored the first Quechua grammar" in 1560 "argues that the native language was comparable to Spanish or Latin and thus acceptable for teaching Christian doctrine" (José de Acosta, *Natural and Moral History*, 257, note 3).

[44] Acosta, *Natural and Moral History*, 257.

the weakness and incompleteness of the indigenous knowledge of God. As further confirmation of indigenous knowledge of God, Acosta adds the evidence of a "very splendid temple," even though that temple was a site of contention between authentic worship of the Creator and idolatrous worship of the devil.[45]

Much more could be written about Acosta's complex and fascinating book, but this would sidetrack us from focusing on what Fray Luis learned about the Americas and their indigenous peoples from his reading of the *Historia*. Before moving forward, though, one further observation is in order, noting what Acosta had to say in the Prologue to what follows after book four. He explains, "Now that I have dealt with things pertaining to the natural history of the Indies, the remaining books will treat its moral history: that is, the customs and deeds of the Indians." The aim of the *Historia*, after all,

> is not only to inform of what is happening in the Indies, but to dedicate that information to the benefit that knowledge of such things can bring, which is to help these peoples to their salvation and to glorify the Creator and Redeemer who led them out of the profound darkness of their heathen beliefs, and imparted to them the wonderful light of his Gospel.[46]

Before embarking on his presentation of the "moral history" of the Indies, Acosta offers a word of caution:

> If any reader is astonished by some of the Indians' rites and customs, and scorns them as ignorant and wicked or detests them as inhuman and diabolical, let him look

---

[45] Acosta also devotes attention to temples erected by indigenous peoples in book five, chapter twelve, "Of the temples that have been found in the Indies," and chapter thirteen, "Of the splendid temples of Mexico."

[46] Acosta, *Natural and Moral History*, 250.

to the Greeks and Romans, who ruled the world, and he will find the same or very similar customs, and sometimes worse ones.[47]

By reading Acosta's book attentively so that he could responsibly discharge his responsibility as its censor, Fray Luis acquired a wealth of information about America and its indigenous peoples. We do not know if he appreciated or even recognized the specifically Ignatian spirituality that permeates Acosta's book. Even so, when Fray Luis wrote that the reader of the *Historia* would be inspired to give praise to God "who is so wonderful in all his works" it is clear that the Jesuit made it possible for his Augustinian censor to see God in all things American as Acosta so extensively catalogued and explained them. To shed further light on what else Fray Luis knew and what he thought about the Americas, we turn to several of his own writings.

What Fray Luis Wrote about the Americas

While the lines Fray Luis penned for Acosta's *Historia natural y moral de las Indias* offered a brief but fervent endorsement of the Jesuit's work, the genre of the *nihil obstat* did not provide him with the latitude that would have made it possible to express his own views more extensively about the Spanish colonial project in the Americas, about the indigenous peoples of the Americas, or about the efforts of missionaries to Christianize them. The attention Fray Luis devotes to the *Conquista* in his own writings shows that his reading of Acosta's *Historia* was not his first exposure to these issues and the energetic debates they inspired in academic and ecclesiastical circles in Spain. The fact that his extensive body of writing does not include many pages devoted to these matters should not

---

[47] Acosta, *Natural and Moral History*, 251.

mislead us to conclude either that Fray Luis was uninformed or that he was indifferent to what was happening across the ocean.

In their translation into Spanish of four Latin works of Fray Luis in which he addresses the "discovery" of America, Andrés Moreno Mengíbar and Juan Martos Fernández insist that this theme receives his attention more frequently than some have assumed, and that this was the case from his earliest days as a professor at the University of Salamanca up until weeks before his death.[48]

As early as the academic years 1567–1568 and 1568–1569 Fray Luis included a consideration of whether violence was permissible in the conquest of America and the evangelization of its indigenous inhabitants in the course *De Fide*, taught as holder of the Durandus chair at Salamanca.[49] At Salamanca, Fray Luis was well positioned to address the arguments that had been proposed on the evangelization of the Americas, and in *De Fide* he demonstrates his familiarity with the debates between las Casas and Sepúlveda that took place at Valladolid in 1550–1551.[50] Moreno Mengíbar and Martos Fernández

---

[48] Andrés Moreno Mengíbar and Juan Martos Fernández, *Fray Luis de León: Escritos sobre América: Estudio preliminar, traducción y notas* (Madrid: Editorial Tecnos, 1999), xviii. The four Latin works translated and discussed by Moreno Mengibar and Martos Fernández are the treatise *De Fide* (1567–1569), the commentary on Job (1575–1591), the commentary on the Song of Songs (1589), and the commentary on Obadiah (1589). On what Fray Luis wrote about the Spanish "discovery" of America also see Andrés Moreno Mengíbar and Juan Martos Fernández, "Mesianismo y Nuevo Mundo en fray Luis de León: *in Abdiam Prophetam Expositio*," *Bulletin Hispanique* 98 (1996): 261–289; Luciano Pereña Vicente, "El descubrimiento de América en las obras de Fray Luis de León," *Revista Española de derecho internacional* 8 (1955): 587–604; Brian Yates, "El Tratado sobre la fe: El argumento de Fray Luis de León sobre el uso de la fuerza para evangelizar a los indios," *Dissidences* 3, no. 5 (2012), Article 8, https://digitalcommons.bowdoin.edu/dissidences/vol3/iss5/8.

[49] *De Fide*, essentially the lecture notes of Fray Luis, was not published until 1893. See Yates, "El Tratado sobre la fe."

[50] See Lewis Hanke, *All Mankind Is One: A Study of the Disputation*

point out that, along with Francisco de Vitoria, the founder of the school of Salamanca, and in agreement with las Casas, Fray Luis taught that the use of force could not be justified inasmuch as the indigenous peoples were "infidels" who had never heard the Gospel. Their sins could not be considered offenses against a faith with which they were entirely unfamiliar. The indigenous peoples of America should not be compelled to accept Christianity because that would result in inauthentic conversions accomplished merely for the sake of convenience. Only patient and gradual evangelization by way of example and not under the threat of arms would be appropriate and truly effective.[51]

In his essay on *De Fide*, Brian Yates points out not only that it has received relatively little attention from students of Fray Luis, but also that scholars are divided on the question of whether Fray Luis agreed with las Casas who opposed the use of force or with Sepúlveda. Yates himself concludes that Fray Luis was of two minds, in some places siding with las Casas and in others with Sepúlveda.[52] For example, in the second part of the treatise, Fray Luis sets forth the argument that "if there are infidels who are so barbaric that they live like animals and whose only law is their instinct, they may be forced by arms to abandon their savage condition and to live like people."[53] He also writes that "Infidels who are the subjects of Christian princes can be forced to separate themselves from the worship of idols and to observe the natural law."[54] While entering into a detailed analysis about the side on which Fray Luis ultimately lands is beyond the scope of this chapter, it

---

between *Bartolomé de Las Casas and Juan Ginés de Sepúlveda in 1550 on the Intellectual and Religious Capacity of the American Indians* (DeKalb: Northern Illinois University Press, 1974).

[51] Moreno Mengíbar and Martos Fernández, *Fray Luis de León*, xviii–xix. On the arguments of Fray Luis in *De Fide*, see Yates, "El Tratado sobre la fe."

[52] Yates, "El Tratado sobre la fe."

[53] Moreno Mengíbar and Martos Fernández, *Fray Luis de León*, 20.

[54] Moreno Mengíbar and Martos Fernández, *Fray Luis de León*, 20.

is enough to register that the attention he gave to the question itself from his professorial cathedra in 1567–1568 and 1568–1569 leaves no doubt as to his familiarity with the issues at stake in the debate and their importance.

Further evidence in support of the argument by Moreno Mengíbar and Martos Fernández that what they call *la tematica americana* was a recurrent concern in the writings of Fray Luis can be found in *The Names of Christ*, which has been called "one of the greatest masterpieces of Renaissance philosophical and spiritual thought."[55] Begun by Fray Luis during the years of his imprisonment while on trial before the Inquisition and first published in 1583, the book is framed as a conversation among three Augustinian friars, Marcelo, Sabino, and Juliano, in which they reflect on names of Christ that are found in the Bible (Bud, Face of God, Way, Shepherd, Mountain, Everlasting Father, Arm of God, King of God, Prince of Peace, Husband, Son of God, Lamb of God, Beloved, Jesus).[56]

During their conversation on "Arm of God," Marcelo tells Juliano and Sabino: "I am convinced that the conversion to Christianity of the diverse nations of the world proves the truth of our religion without any possible doubt and destroys completely the reasoning of infidels, no matter how clever."[57] Marcelo then tells his companions:

> What took place in the past throughout the Roman Empire is also taking place today in the New World recently discovered, where the holy gospels are displayed

---

[55] Luis de León, *The Names of Christ*, 1.

[56] Moreno Mengíbar and Martos Fernández suggest that there has been insufficient attention to the influence on *The Names of Christ* of Jewish traditions of reflection on the names of God and the meaning of the Tetragrammaton (*Fray Luis de León, Escritos sobre América*, xx). "Bud," the first of the names of Christ, is the English translation of the Spanish "pimpollo," as in the bud of a flower.

[57] Luis de León, *The Names of Christ*, 182.

in flags of victory and idol worship is being stamped out. The spread of Christianity is due to either the power of God, or to the forces of evil, and we must now conclude that the Devil is bound to fight such an enterprise, since it weakens him. We see in it, therefore, inescapably the strength of God's arm.[58]

The voice of Fray Luis is unmistakable here. Luciano Pereña Vicente says that for Fray Luis, the Spanish "discovery" of the Americas was the greatest event that centuries had ever known.[59] One key question that arises from this finds expression in chapter fifteen of book one of Acosta's *Historia*: "it is certain that the Holy Spirit knew all of these secrets far in advance, and it seems a very reasonable supposition that there would be some mention in Holy Writ of a matter as great as the discovery and conversion to the Faith of Christ of the New World."[60] The quest for a connection between biblical prophecy and the "discovery" of the New World began with Columbus in 1492, and Fray Luis himself addressed this connection in three of his commentaries on biblical texts.[61] These are his Commentary on Job (1575–1591), the (Latin) Commentary on the Song of Songs (1589), and the Commentary on Obadiah (1589). Perhaps coincidentally, the latter two were published in 1589, the year in which Fray Luis dates his review of Acosta's *Historia*. While Job and the Song of Songs might seem unlikely places to find prophetic predictions for anything at all, both are books to which Fray Luis devoted considerable attention throughout his career.[62]

---

[58] Luis de León, *The Names of Christ*, 183.

[59] Pereña Vicente, "El descubrimiento de América," 587–588.

[60] José de Acosta, *Natural and Moral History of the Indies*, 50.

[61] See Ruiz, *Readings from the Edges*, 123–139: "The Bible and the Exegesis of Empire" on the *Book of Prophecies* of Christopher Columbus.

[62] According to Moreno Mengíbar and Martos Fernández, Fray

Fray Luis began work on his commentary on Job in 1575 while imprisoned during his trial before the Inquisition and only completed it in 1591, the year of his death. In his consideration of chapter twenty-eight, the poem on wisdom, Fray Luis finds correspondences between the biblical text and the New World. According to Fray Luis, in Job 28:4 (*"Dividit torrens a populo pere-grinante eos quos oblitus est pes egentis hominis, et invios,"* according to the Vulgate), "pilgrim people" refers to Spaniards, who "travel far from their lands and their homes, and who by their navigation have gone around the globe."[63] In 28:10 he finds a reference to the silver mines at Potosí (then Peru, now Bolivia) and the wealth that they produced.

In his 1589 Latin commentary on the Song of Songs, Fray Luis finds a hidden reference to America in 8:8. In the Vulgate, this verse reads, *"Soror nostra parva, et ubera non habet; quid faciemus sorori nostrae in die quando alloquenda est?"* ("We have a little sister, and she has no breasts. What shall we do for our sister, on the day when she is spoken for?" *NRSV*). According to Fray Luis,

> The image of this younger and not very beautiful sister . . . represents many peoples and nations far removed from our world who must be led to Christ with a new way of transmitting the Gospel: that is, it represents the recently

---

Luis was the first to explore what they call a "providentialist" reading of historical events and their foretelling in the pages of the book of Job (*Fray Luis de León, Escritos sobre América*, xxiii). They point out that while the Flemish scholar Frans Titelmans (1502–1537) had pointed to Job 28:4 as a reference to distant peoples who were lost and unknown, it was Fray Luis who identified these as the indigenous people of the Americas (*Fray Luis de León, Escritos sobre América*, xxiii–xxxiv).

63 Moreno Mengíbar and Martos Fernández, *Fray Luis de León, Escritos sobre América*, 29. This and subsequent translations from this text are mine.

accomplished conversion to faith in Christ of the world discovered by the Spanish in their navigations to the faith of Christ.[64]

In his comment on Song 8:9 we learn about how the Augustinian scholar regarded the indigenous peoples of the newly discovered lands, and about his preoccupation with the violence that accompanied evangelization. The Vulgate version of this verse reads "*Si murus est, aedificemus super eum propugnacula argentea; si ostium est, compingamus illud tabulis cedrinis*" ("If she is a wall, we will build upon her a battlement of silver; but if she is a door, we will enclose her with boards of cedar" *NRSV*). In his allegorical reading of this verse, Fray Luis explains

> Christ affirms that, when the time comes for the conversion of these nations, it is necessarily to skillfully correct what is lacking or imperfect in them . . . he declares how he will act by using two metaphors which, if we examine them attentively, will reveal the character of those nations and the whole process of converting them to Christ. For, first of all, some of these nations are completely wild and savage and extremely obstinate . . . these he rightly calls 'wall' because of the hardness of their hearts and their customs, which cannot be tamed in any way. On the other hand, there are others who are so docile by nature that they can be led anywhere without any effort, and they are frank and simple and their character above all naïve and peaceable. So, these can be compared to a door.[65]

---

[64] Moreno Mengíbar and Martos Fernández, *Fray Luis de León, Escritos sobre América*, 39.

[65] Moreno Mengíbar and Martos Fernández, *Fray Luis de León, Escritos sobre América*, 42.

Addressing what the Song of Songs has to say about the use of force in the Christianization of the peoples of America, Fray Luis writes that "In the conversion of these nations to Christ, force was used to a certain extent, because the Gospel was not announced to them by defenseless people, as it was in the past, but by armed men, or at least by those who were protected by armed people as they transmitted pious doctrine to them."[66] He claims that Song 8:9 foretold this as well, because neither a wall nor a door can be built without using iron and without employing force.

Fray Luis concludes this section with an apocalyptic turn, arguing that while these texts allude to the Church and its activity in the present time, they also point toward the last days, which are imminent: "once the Gospel has been announced to the whole world and all peoples have been incorporated into the Church, in the final moment of the world and of the Church, the Jews must be converted to faith in Christ, and after their conversion the world will come to an end."[67] For Fray Luis and for many of his contemporaries, the task of converting the indigenous peoples of the New World to Christianity had a special urgency—even to the extent

---

[66] Moreno Mengíbar and Martos Fernández, *Fray Luis de León, Escritos sobre América*, 43. In a footnote, Moreno Mengíbar and Martos Fernández point out that here, as in *De Fide*, Fray Luis expresses concern over the counterproductive effects of violence on the possible success of Spanish efforts at evangelization.

[67] Moreno Mengíbar and Martos Fernández, *Fray Luis de León, Escritos sobre América*, 44. Apocalyptic anxiety does not develop in a political vacuum. Moreno Mengíbar and Martos Fernández explain that Fray Luis could not avoid being influenced by the apocalyptic currents that were circulating in Castile between 1587 and 1588, precipitated by dire economic circumstances, by the preparations for the sailing of the Armada and its dramatic defeat, and by significant reversals in foreign policy (*Fray Luis de León, Escritos sobre América*, xxxii). On the apocalypticism of Fray Luis, see Karl A. Kottman, *Law and Apocalypse: The Moral Thought of Luis de León (1527?–1591)* (The Hague: Martinus Nijhoff, 1972).

that the otherwise unacceptable use of force was countenanced—because this would be among the catalysts that would lead to the second coming of Christ.

It was also in 1589 that Fray Luis published his commentary on Obadiah. There he finds a connection between prophecy and the Spanish discovery of the New World in verse 20, which reads, according to the Vulgate, "*et transmigratio Hierusalem, quae in Bosphora est, possidebit civitares austri,*" "and the exiles of Jerusalem, who are in the Bosporus, will inherit the cities of the south." In his interpretation of this text, Fray Luis takes issue with the Vulgate's rendering of *Bosphora*, preferring the Hebrew *Sefarad* instead, and insisting that Obadiah intended this as a reference to Spain.[68] In the Hebrew Bible, this place-name occurs only in Obadiah 20 and its identification is entirely uncertain.[69] On the basis of this identification, which is in fact the traditional Jewish designation for Spain, Fray Luis exclaims:

> we must establish that, no matter how much we review
> the entire history of times past, we will not find anything
> that is, nor has anything happened so unexpectedly than
> what happened in the time of our parents when Spaniards,
> navigating the vast ocean, found a new world, no less than
> the Roman world but possibly more extensive and greater.
> In effect, no one thought that there might be other lands,

---

[68] Moreno Mengíbar and Martos Fernández, *Fray Luis de León, Escritos sobre América*, 69–77. Moreno Mengíbar and Martos Fernández point out that Fray Luis does not hesitate to refute the unassailable authority of Saint Jerome, demonstrating how confused he was by translating the Hebrew term as "Bosphorus" (*Fray Luis de León, Escritos sobre América*, xxviii).

[69] See Mariona Vernel Pons, "The Origin of the Name Sepharad: A New Interpretation," *Journal of Semitic Studies* 59 (2014): 297–313. Also see David Weissert, "Obadiah 20: Septuagint and Vulgate," *Textus* 24 (2009): 85–106.

apart from the ones we inhabit, and even if someone may have suspected it, no one would believe that people could live or visit there.[70]

In what seems to be a curious coincidence José de Acosta also interprets Obadiah 20 as a prophetic prediction of Spain's discovery of America and the Christianization of its indigenous peoples. Chapter fifteen of book one of the *Historia*, entitled "Of the prophecy of Abdias, which some say concerned these Indies," begins "There are some who say and affirm that a long time ago it was prophesied in Holy Writ that this New World would be converted to Christ, and by people of Spain. And in support of this they quote the ending of the prophecy of Abdias."[71] He proceeds to defend this view against any criticism:

> Whoever wishes to declare the prophecy of Abdias in this form should not be blamed, for it is certain that the Holy Spirit knew all of these secrets far in advance, and it seems a very reasonable supposition that there would be some mention in Holy Writ of a matter as great as the discovery and conversion to the Faith of Christ of the New World.[72]

In the same chapter we find Acosta expressing apocalyptic expectations quite similar to those of Fray Luis, a clear indication that the Augustinian was not alone in advancing such views. According to Acosta, "For what the Savior so strongly impressed on us, that the Gospel will be preached to the whole world and then shall the consummation come, surely states that as long as the world lasts there will be people in it who have not received news

---

[70] Moreno Mengíbar and Martos Fernández, *Fray Luis de León, Escritos sobre América*, 49.

[71] Acosta, *Natural and Moral History of the Indies*, 49.

[72] Acosta, *Natural and Moral History of the Indies*, 50.

of Christ."[73] It was this understanding of the imminence of the "consummation" that made the Christianization of the indigenous peoples of the Americas such an urgent imperative both for the Jesuit and for the Augustinian.

In an essay entitled "Fray Luis and the Concern with Language," Carlos G. Noreña argues that the eschatological views of Fray Luis combine into an "amazing apocalyptic vision two historical facts of his time: the supposed conversion of the Spanish Jews after 1492 and the preaching of the Gospel in the Americas by Spanish missionaries."[74] According to Noreña, "That the end of the world would be immediately preceded by the conversion of the Jews to Christianity was a widespread belief based on a rather fanciful interpretation of some biblical quotations."[75] It is what Moreno Mengíbar and Martos Fernández call his *obsesión escatológica indiana*[76] that accounts for the fact that "Fray Luis accepted the opinion of those who maintained that the American Indians could and should be coerced into civilization and Christianity by the power of Spain," as Noreña points out. Noreña laments that even though Fray Luis sometimes "solemnly deplored the greed and unnecessary cruelty of the Conquistadores," he "succumbed tragically to the bias of his historical environment."[77] Noreña's eyebrow-raising assessment of Fray Luis's turn to the Bible is worth noting:

> To make things worse Fray Luis came out with an almost ridiculous interpretation of some Biblical texts to "prove" that the Spanish conquest of the Americas had been

---

[73] Acosta, *Natural and Moral History of the Indies*, 50–51.

[74] Carlos G. Noreña, *Studies in Spanish Renaissance Thought* (The Hague: Martinus Nijhoff, 1975), 159. Also see Moreno Mengíbar and Martos Fernández, *Fray Luis de León, Escritos sobre América*, xviii.

[75] Noreña, *Studies in Spanish Renaissance Thought*, 159.

[76] Moreno Mengíbar and Martos Fernández, *Fray Luis de León, Escritos sobre América*, xxi.

[77] Noreña, *Studies in Spanish Renaissance Thought*, 159.

clearly revealed [sic!] by God through Isaiah and Job.
Furthermore, it was his contention that in the book of
Abdias God Himself had revealed the choice of Spain
for this formidable task of discovering, colonizing, and
converting the American Indians. . . . This misleading
effort . . . culminated in the supreme folly of engaging in
detailed Bibliomancy with the solemn prognostication of
the end of the world by, exactly, 1656. Fray Luis' obviously
unfulfilled prophecy is perfectly in tune with all the apocalyptic, cabalistic, messianic, magical, and astrological fads
of his age, and reveals the strange combination of enlightenment and naiveté which characterizes the sixteenth
century in Europe.[78]

"Dios te perdone," the Spanish language inscription left by a
visitor to Cave 18 on Mona Island might appropriately be invoked
for the sake of Fray Luis in view of his judgment that indigenous
peoples could and should be coerced into accepting Christianity.
Yet it is equally fitting as a response to Noreña's much less than
moderate verdict on how Fray Luis interpreted the Bible.[79]

In a more measured assessment of what Fray Luis had to say
about Obadiah 20, Thompson observes that the Augustinian

---

[78] Noreña, *Studies in Spanish Renaissance Thought*, 159. Thompson
points out that the claim by some (Noreña among them) that Fray Luis
predicted that the world would end in 1656 are mistaken, because "he
rejected any such certainty or even the attempt to do more than read the
signs" (Colin P. Thompson, *The Strife of Tongues: Fray Luis de León and the
Golden Age of Spain* [Cambridge: Cambridge University Press, 1988], 103).

[79] Scholars have paid close attention to the serious engagement of
Fray Luis (and his sixteenth century contemporaries, among them Teresa
de Ávila and Juan de la Cruz) with Kabbala. See, for example, Catherine
Swietlicki, *Spanish Christian Cabala: The Works of Luis de León, Santa
Teresa de Jesús and San Juan de la Cruz* (Columbia: University of Missouri
Press, 1986).

expresses wonder at the vastness of the territories discovered, the multitudes of their inhabitants who have hitherto
dwelt in darkness, and the achievements of those Spaniards
who have undertaken perilous journeys over a greater area
than the Romans ever covered. The Gospel, it was thought,
had been preached to all [*human*]kind, yet here are peoples
who have never heard even a whisper of it.[80]

Thus, the answer of Fray Luis to the silence of Scripture about
the discovery of the Americas by Spain was to deny that silence.[81]
There should be no reason for Fray Luis himself to seek *a poste-
riori* absolution for the ways in which his own practices of biblical
interpretation reflected the spirit of the times in which he lived, in
all their complexity. At the same time, it would be inappropriately
anachronistic to evaluate his interpretation of the Bible in twenty-
first-century terms.[82] We cannot and should not pretend that
Fray Luis was interested in interreligious dialogue with the indigenous peoples of the Americas. Nothing could be further from the
truth. Luis de León was preoccupied with their Christianization,
and he shared with his contemporaries the view that the Spanish

---

[80] Thompson, *The Strife of Tongues*, 99.

[81] Thompson, *The Strife of Tongues*, 100.

[82] Thompson usefully instructs, with respect to Fray Luis and his
interpretation of Obadiah 20, that "What is so disconcerting to a twen-
tieth-century reader" of Fray Luis "is the mixture of the fanciful and the
arbitrary on the one hand, and the step-by-step internal logic of his method
on the other hand. When he is describing the voyages to the New World
and the nature of its inhabitants he is matter-of-fact and is reflecting what
he has read and heard" (including from José de Acosta). "The way he relates
this to words and images in the Biblical text . . . is alien to us. Nonetheless,
it is important to grasp that though some of his exegesis may have been
original, he was working within well-defined traditions and was used to
making connections between words and concepts, language and thought,
which will elude us" (*The Strife of Tongues*, 101).

missionaries in the Americas were taking sides in an apocalyptic battle between God and Satan on soil far from their homeland. A Spanish and Christian victory in that battle, as Fray Luis and many of his contemporaries firmly believed, would set the stage for the glorious return of Christ and the end of the present age. If coercion was required to accomplish the conversion of indigenous Americans, Fray Luis considered it lamentable but necessary.

The characterization of Fray Luis's biblical interpretation as "almost ridiculous" and as a matter of "detailed Bibliomancy" that reveals a "strange combination of enlightenment and naiveté" might leave a reader doubtful as to whether anything of lasting value can be retrieved from the work of Fray Luis. While his approach to biblical interpretation certainly reflects the spirit of sixteenth-century Spain in all its complexity, his defense of Spanish (vs. Latin) as a fitting language for translation of the Bible and his emphasis on the significance of the Incarnation of the Word converge in important and distinctive ways. It is to that convergence that we now turn.

Convergences:
Fray Luis on the Vernacular and the Incarnation

In Defense of the Vernacular

In the dedication of book three of *The Names of Christ*, addressed to Pedro Portocarrero, Fray Luis grumbled about how some readers had expressed unfavorable opinions about the first two books.[83] He complained that

---

[83] Pedro Portocarrero, identified in the dedication as "del Consejo de Su Majestad y General Inquisición," a friend of Fray Luis, was twice rector of the University of Salamanca (1556–1557 and 1566–1567). See Fray Luis de León, *Obras Completas Castellanas*, vol. 1, p. 405, note 1.

Some readers expected from its author, a theologian, a
learned treatise in Latin, and found it disappointing that
my book was written in Spanish [*en romance*]. According
to other readers Spanish [*romance*] is not the right
language to write about rather deep philosophical matters,
since many readers may be incapable of following the
chain of reasoning included in the text. Some claim they
would have read the text if written in Latin, but will refuse
to read it simply because I wrote it in Spanish.[84]

He responded to these critics energetically, though not
without a sense of humor, writing, "I want my friends to feel happy
with my work, my enemies to feel less happy about their reproaches
to my work."[85] Fray Luis argued that

it is a common mistake to despise a text simply because it
is written in a modern language such as Spanish, not in
Latin, Greek, and so forth. Spanish can express the loft-
iest thoughts. We often misuse it out of ignorance, yet

---

[84] *The Names of Christ*, 265. "Unos se maravillan que un teólogo,
de quien, como ellos dicen, esperaban algunos grandes tratados llenos de
profundas cuestiones, haya salido a la fin con un libro en romance. Otros
dicen que no eran para romance las cosas que se tratan en estos libros,
porque no son capaces de ellas todos los que entienden romance. Y otros
hay que no los han querido leer, porque están en su lengua; y dicen que, si
estuvieran en latín, los leyeran" (Fray Luis de León, Los nombres de Cristo,
in *Obras Completas Castellanas I*, fifth revised edition (Madrid: Biblioteca
de Autores Cristianos, 1991), 685. Fray Luis was also aware of the criticism
he received from readers of his book, *The Perfect Wife* (*La perfecta casada*),
which he also wrote in Spanish. He mentions the opinion of some who
judged him unqualified to write such a work, "because of my calling and
because of the fact that I am not married, to tell married women how they
should act and behave" (*The Names of Christ*, 265).

[85] *The Names of Christ*, 265.

this is our fault, not the fault of the Spanish language nor
the fault of those writers who strive to bend and shape
the Spanish language so that it can convey lofty and
exquisite ideas.[86]

He accused his detractors of elitism, asking if was possible
"that they do not want other readers to understand me, thinking
that only a few understand Latin, and so the other readers will
have to remain ignorant of what I have to say?"[87] It was hardly the
case that Fray Luis was incapable of writing in Latin. He authored
works of dogmatic theology and biblical commentaries in Latin,
and yet Noreña (the same Noreña who accused Fray Luis of the
"almost ridiculous interpretation of some biblical texts" and of
"Bibliomancy") declares that "The two books, published by Fray
Luis in 1583," that is, *The Names of Christ* and *The Perfect Wife*,
"opened a new era in the history of Spanish spiritual literature in
the vernacular."[88] Such publications were audacious for, as Noreña
also points out, "Any vernacular publication stressing the inner
character of religious life or making the Bible available to the
masses of the faithful was considered dangerous, and was consequently labeled as Lutheran, Calvinistic, or at least, Erasmian
. . . the Tribunal of the Inquisition went to work with amazing
enthusiasm."[89] Fray Luis came to know the "amazing enthusiasm"
of the Inquisition through his own arduous experience of years of
incarceration while on trial. Noreña also points out that "Up until
1601 the University of Salamanca," where Fray Luis studied and
taught, "had to fight the attempt of some Dominican theologians

---

[86] *The Names of Christ*, 265–266.

[87] *The Names of Christ*, 266.

[88] Noreña, *Studies in Spanish Renaissance Thought*, 164.

[89] Noreña, *Studies in Spanish Renaissance Thought*, 164. See Marcel
Bataillon, *Erasmo y España: estudios sobre la historia spiritual del siglo xvi*,
2nd Spanish edition (México: Fondo de Cultura Económica, 1966.)

to forbid without exception the publication of any vernacular book dealing with any religious matter whatsoever."[90]

Fray Luis was merciless in rebutting his critics:

> Some readers are snobbish enough to state that they do not read my books because they were written in the Spanish language and claim they would read them if they had been written in Latin. They are lazy enough with respect to their mother tongue: They have made no contribution to it and always talk about other languages. I claim that they should come to terms with their own language, which certainly they know better than the Latin language, even if they are weak in their knowledge of the Spanish language, which is true in most cases.[91]

Beside this withering *ad hominem* attack, Fray Luis answered his detractors by contending that "with respect to languages there is no basic difference among them, there are no languages that should be held in reserve and used only for certain subjects. Each and every language is capable of expressing the whole range of human knowledge."[92] Nodding in the direction of the unassailable classics of Greece and Rome in support of his views on common, vernacular language, he pointed out that "Plato wrote uncommon, exquisite thoughts in what was then the common language of Greece. Cicero did the same in what was then, when he was alive, the common language of the Romans," not missing the opportunity to make it clear that Latin had once been (but no longer was) anyone's mother tongue.[93] He added mention of Saints Basil, John Chrysostom, Gregory of Nazianzen, and Cyril, pointing out how

---

[90] Noreña, *Studies in Spanish Renaissance Thought*, 165.
[91] *The Names of Christ*, 267.
[92] *The Names of Christ*, 266.
[93] *The Names of Christ*, 266–267.

in their Greek mother tongue, "which at the time when they were alive children drank in along with their milk and saleswomen spoke in the plaza, they wrote about the most divine mysteries of our faith, and they did not hesitate to put in their language what they knew would not be comprehended by many of those who understood the language."[94]

Commenting on these lines, Geneviève Fabry recognizes how for Fray Luis, "the mother tongue is the language of exchanges, be they nutritional, commercial or affective: for Fray Luis, language is a liquid that children imbibe along with their milk. In general, we might affirm that this markedly oral and affective language is also one that founds a full and carnal listening, an incarnate listening."[95] Other mystical writers of sixteenth-century Spain, namely Teresa de Ávila and Juan de la Cruz, echo this. Fabry explains that Luis de León explicitly established a link between the legitimacy of the use of a language for intellectual purposes and the learning of that language during childhood.[96]

Given what he wrote in defense of his own use of Spanish, that "each and every language is capable of expressing the whole range of human knowledge," how might Fray Luis have answered in the light of what he wrote? How might Fray Luis have countered what he read in the pages of Acosta's *Historia* where the Jesuit remarked (as mentioned above) that the indig-

---

[94] "Los santos Basilio y Crisóstomo y Gregorio Nacianceno y Cirilo, con toda la antigüedad de los griegos, en su lengua maternal griega, que, cuando ellos vivían, la mamaban con la leche los niños y la hablaban en la plaza las vendedoras, escribieron los misterioso más divinos de nuestro fe, y no dudaron de poner en su lengua lo que sabían que no había de ser entendido por muchos de los que entendían la lengua" (*Los nombres de Cristo*, 687). Translation mine.

[95] Fabry, "El Cantar de los Cantares en la obra de Luis de León, San Juan de la Cruz y Juan Gelman," 3.

[96] Fabry, "El Cantar de los Cantares en la obra de Luis de León, San Juan de la Cruz y Juan Gelman," 3.

enous peoples of the Americas "have no word of their own
with which to name God," and so, "those who preach or write
for the Indians use our Spanish word *Dios*."[97] What might
the Augustinian have written in response to the conclusion
at which his Jesuit contemporary arrived on the basis of this
observation, namely, that the deficiency he had perceived in
indigenous languages demonstrated the "weak and incomplete
knowledge they have of God"?[98] Perhaps, if his role as censor
did not impose limits on what Fray Luis could or could not
permit himself to say, we can imagine that he may have chided
Acosta as he did his own detractors, by suggesting that Acosta
reached this conclusion based on inadequate and inaccurate
knowledge of the indigenous vernaculars. Perhaps, Fray Luis
might even have written, greater familiarity with their vernacular languages might have led the learned Jesuit to a different
judgment about the knowledge of God in America. Noreña
writes that "Spanish missionaries," Acosta among them, "played
a decisive part in reporting the linguistic characteristics of the
American Indians," and that the "struggle of the vernacular had
also a distinctly Spanish flavor in that it was intimately associated with the problems of regional separatism and the birth
of a truly national consciousness."[99] Language was a lively issue
in sixteenth-century Spain! Unfortunately, we do not know
whether or not Fray Luis, energetic advocate on behalf of the
Spanish vernacular that he was, had any familiarity with the
indigenous languages of the Americas besides what he may have
read and what he may have heard.

    For what reasons did Fray Luis mount such a vigorous
defense of his use of Spanish in *The Names of Christ*? As Colin

---

[97] Acosta, *Natural and Moral History*, 257.

[98] Acosta, *Natural and Moral History*, 257.

[99] Noreña, *Studies in Spanish Renaissance Thought*, 187.

P. Thompson explains, Fray Luis "valued and loved the Bible so much that he wrote the *Names* to compensate as far as possible for the fact that the glories of Christ in Scripture were forbidden to literate lay people who could not read Latin."[100] The same motive—making the Bible accessible and understandable to those who could not read Latin—led him to translate the Song of Songs into Spanish and to provide a Spanish-language commentary. Produced between 1561 and 1562 when Fray Luis was only thirty-three years old, this was his first biblical commentary. He produced this work specifically for his cousin Isabel Osorio, who was a nun in the *Espiritu Santo* convent in Salamanca, and Fray Luis did not intend for it to be published.[101] Despite that intention, it circulated widely enough to draw considerable attention to him, a good bit of it critical. According to Noreña, "the manuscript leaked to the public and soon hundreds of copies were circulated not only among students of the University but throughout Spain and even in the American colonies.[102] His authorship of a Spanish translation and commentary on the Song of Songs was among the charges levelled against Fray Luis that resulted in his arrest by functionaries of the Inquisition on March 27, 1572.[103] These included the accusation that Fray Luis

---

[100] Colin P. Thompson, Review of *Luis de León: The Names of Christ*, in *New Blackfriars* 66, no. 778 (April 1985): 201. Noreña also says about *The Names of Christ* that "As a theological treatise the book represents the most harmonious synthesis of Biblical, Patristic, and speculative theology ever written by the disciples of Vitoria and Melchor Cano. Through this book biblical poetry, primitive Christianity, and solid scholastic theology became the spiritual nourishment of Spanish Catholics outside the University classrooms, the simple Christian folk uninformed and uninterested in the annoying theological controversies of rival professors" (*Studies in Spanish Renaissance Thought*, 168).

[101] Thompson, *The Strife of Tongues*, 26.

[102] Noreña, *Studies in Spanish Renaissance Thought*, 193.

[103] Thompson, *The Strife of Tongues*, 36.

held "that the Song of Songs is a love song by Solomon to the daughter of Pharaoh, and to teach otherwise is futile," and that "the Song of Songs can be read and explained in the vernacular language."[104]

Fabry explains that Fray Luis countered "with a certain malice," those who criticized him for writing about the Song of Songs in Spanish: if one reader was scandalized by reading Spanish words like "kisses" and "embraces" and "breasts" and "clear eyes" that often appear in the Song of Songs, then it is clear that this person had neither read nor understood the Latin version of the Song, in which the very same words appear.[105] In Fabry's view, Fray Luis insisted that it is listening in vernacular language that allows the world of the text to unfold in all its fullness on the emotional, affective, and imaginary planes. In 1580, he finally silenced his detractors by publishing *In Cantica canticorum Solomonis explanatio*, a Latin translation and commentary on the Song of Songs.[106]

The assertion on the part of Fray Luis that there is no basic difference among languages must not be misinterpreted to imply that this poet and theologian and biblical scholar was indifferent to languages in their variety and their particularity. Nothing could be further from the truth because language mattered a great deal to Fray Luis. Colin P. Thompson recog-

---

[104] Ángel Alcalá, ed., *Proceso Inquisitorial de Fray Luis de León* (Salamanca: Junta de Castilla y León, Consejería de Cultura y Turismo, 2009), xxxii. This enormous (close to eight hundred pages) and enormously useful volume contains the *acta* of the trial of Fray Luis before the Inquisition at Valladolid.

[105] Fabry, "El Cantar de los Cantares en la obra de Luis de León, San Juan de la Cruz y Juan Gelman," 3. María Martín Gómez explains in detail how, for Fray Luis, translation was a form of interpretation (*La Escuela de Salamanca*, 57–69).

[106] Fabry, "El Cantar de los Cantares en la obra de Luis de León, San Juan de la Cruz y Juan Gelman," 3.

nizes the Spanish commentary on the Song of Songs as an early example of the interest in Fray Luis "in the theology of language . . . the language of divine revelation."[107] According to Thompson,

> If metaphor properly understood could be for Fray Luis a means of ascent towards God, then the language of the Bible and all its figures of speech would show the corresponding process, the divine descent to humanity. By speaking through the words of Scripture God reaches down to the human level and communicates in a manner suited to human limitations. Biblical language is itself a kind of incarnation.[108]

This theology of language, bound up the importance of the incarnation in the thinking of Fray Luis, is what made it vitally important for him to defend the fact that he chose to write in Spanish—his own vernacular—even though he was equally capable of writing in Latin. It is to that connection between the theology of language and the incarnation in the thinking of Fray Luis that we will turn in the next section of this chapter. For the moment, though, it is important to note that the battle between Spanish and Latin in which Fray Luis was engaged, and as a result of which he found himself on trial before the Inquisition, was no mere matter of aesthetic preferences or personal preferences, or even of academic snobbery vis-à-vis the less sophisticated modes of expression of the laity.

The sixteenth-century battle over vernacular languages versus Latin was both political and ecclesiastical in Spain and elsewhere in Europe, a high stakes contest about authority. In the dedication

---

[107] Thompson, *The Strife of Tongues*, 26.
[108] Thompson, *The Strife of Tongues*, 26.

at the beginning of book one of *The Names of Christ*, Fray Luis demonstrated his awareness of these factors even as he offered a vigorous argument in favor of translating the Bible into the spoken vernaculars of ordinary people. He wrote:

> God inspired the writing of Scripture so that it would be a solace to us amid the trials of life, a clear, unfailing light amid darkness and error, and a salutary remedy for the wounds which sin had inflicted upon our souls. Therefore He intended Scripture to be available for the use of all. To this end, He saw to it that it was written in the plainest language, the ordinary speech of those to whom revealed truth was directed.
>
> When, in later days, the knowledge of Jesus Christ was given to the Gentiles, Sacred Scripture was translated into many tongues so that all could profit by it. Hence, in the early days of the Church, and for many years thereafter, it was considered a grave omission if the faithful did not spend a good part of their time in the study of the Bible. . . .
>
> Yet, although the reading of Scripture is good and useful in itself, it has now become the occasion of much harm, as the condition of our age and recent sad experiences teach us. Hence, those who rule the Church were compelled by circumstances to place definite and precise restrictions on the use of the vernacular so that the Bible would be removed from the hands of the uninstructed who would misuse it.
>
> So far as I can see, this unfortunate situation springs from two causes: ignorance and pride, and perhaps more from pride than from ignorance.[109]

---

[109] Fray Luis de León, *The Names of Christ*, translation adapted from

Fray Luis was well aware of the rulings of the Council of Trent on the authority of the Vulgate and the shadow that the outcome of these debates cast on the translation of the Bible into the languages of Europe, including Spanish. At the Council, as Thompson explains, the Spanish delegation "took a strongly conservative line and Cardinal Pacheco had demanded that every translation of the Bible apart from the Vulgate should be prohibited."[110] Domingo de Soto (1494–1560), a founder of the so-called School of Salamanca, arguing against the Protestant position that the Scriptures could be read by any believer, maintained that "it is not good that the Scriptures be published in Spanish [*en romance*], because while some can be trusted, these are very rare."[111]

In in its decree on the Vulgate (1546), the Council of Trent declared "that the old well known Latin Vulgate edition which has been tested in the church by long use over so many centuries should be kept as the authentic text in public readings, debates, sermons and explanations; and no one is to dare or presume on any pretext to reject it."[112] The reason for this restriction is detailed in the next paragraph of the decree:

> The council further decrees, in order to control those of unbalanced character, that no one, relying on [*their*] personal judgment in matters of faith and customs which are linked to the establishment of Christian doctrine, shall dare to

Noreña, *Studies in Spanish Renaissance Thought*, 194–195.

[110] Thompson, *The Strife of Tongues*, 40. María Martín Gómez points out that Spain was well represented at the Council of Trent, with Domingo de Soto appointed by Emperor Charles V and some sixty-eight other Spaniards accompanying him (*La Escuela de Salamanca, Fray Luis de Leon y el Problema de la Interpretación* [Pamplona: Ediciones Universidad de Navarra, 2017], 22).

[111] Martín Gómez, *La Escuela de Salamanca*, 28.

[112] Translation from Tanner, *Decrees of the Ecumenical Councils*, Volume 2, 664.

interpret the sacred scriptures either by twisting the text to [*their*] individual meaning in opposition to that which has been and is held by holy mother church, whose function is to pass judgment on the true meaning of the sacred scriptures.[113]

Trent's privileging of the Vulgate as the "authentic text" was intended to maintain ecclesiastical control over the interpretation of the Bible, in response to the Protestant reformers' insistence on *sola Scriptura* as authoritative. Yet, as Thompson points out, the Tridentine decree nowhere further specified what was meant by "authentic," "Nor did it pronounce upon the vexed matter of vernacular translations of Scripture."[114] In the aftermath of Trent, with the shadow that this council cast over vernacular translation in the light of the privileging of the Vulgate's authority, the efforts of Fray Luis were daring and dangerous. "It is plain," Thompson tells us, "that Fray Luis regretted the almost total ban on vernacular versions of Scripture," and, as both the reasons that led him to this position, "Both his incarnational view of its language and his defence of its translation in the prologue of the first book of the *Nombres* underline his preoccupation with making Scripture accessible to those who could not read Latin."[115] For Fray Luis as an interpreter of the Bible, Thompson concludes, "The language of Scripture spoke ... with a unique authority. ... Its authority meant that its words were visible signs of divine revelation, often hidden beneath apparently simple images."[116]

With access to the riches of the Bible provided by translations in their own vernacular languages, Fray Luis hoped that ordinary people would no doubt be inspired by their reading "to praise God,

---

[113] Translation from Tanner, *Decrees of the Ecumenical Councils, Volume 2*, 664.

[114] Thompson, *The Strife of Tongues*, 40.

[115] Thompson, *The Strife of Tongues*, 121.

[116] Thompson, *The Strife of Tongues*, 138.

who is so wonderful in all his works," to borrow a line from the *nihil obstat* that he provided for Acosta's *Historia*. As suggested earlier, these words of Fray Luis voice a sentiment that is wholly consonant with the inscription *Plura fecit Deus*, read and understood as praise of God's many works in response to the Taíno vernacular symbols that one sixteenth-century Spanish visitor beheld in Cave 18 on Mona Island. For Fray Luis, appreciation of the power of language in all its variety together with his passion for the Bible and for rendering it broadly accessible were rooted in his emphasis on the centrality of the Incarnation of the Word.

The Impact of the Incarnation

As early as his Spanish translation and commentary on the Song of Songs, Fray Luis foregrounded "his incarnational view of the language of the Bible."[117] As Thompson unpacks the Augustinian's soteriology, God created human beings in the divine image and likeness, becoming Incarnate to redeem humankind. "But already before the Incarnation," God "is revealed in [*God's*] dealings and conversations with [*humans*] throughout the Scriptures . . . in which the care the Holy Spirit takes to be conformed to our style by copying our language by imitating the whole range of our mind and our condition is a wonderful thing."[118]

In his Latin commentary on the Song of Songs, published in 1580, Fray Luis interprets the first verse, "Let him kiss me with the kisses of his mouth! For your love is better than wine" (*NRSV*) as an expression "of the desire of the ancient people of God for the Word to be made incarnate," and so the "Word made flesh is the divine 'kissing' of humanity, and kisses are better than wine because at the Incarnation the Church beholds on earth joys beforehand

---

117 Thompson, *The Strife of Tongues*, 27.
118 Thompson, *The Strife of Tongues*, 27.

only known in heaven."[119] Fray Luis did not hesitate to use the
sensuous imagery of the Song of Songs to describe the ultimate
instance of embodiment, the Incarnation of the Word. In this way,
the Word of God in the text of Scripture gives witness to the Word
of God made flesh in the person of Jesus. With Duns Scotus, Fray
Luis believed that the Incarnation would have taken place even
if the fall of Adam and Eve had not occurred.[120] As Thompson
explains, for Fray Luis, "Everything that God created leads up to
[God's] greatest act, the Incarnation; and the communication of
[*divine*] goodness and perfection to the creatures issues in the
highest gift [*God*] could bestow on creation, the Incarnate Word,
in whom [God's] glory is manifested."[121]

A rich christology was at the heart of the theology directly
and indirectly set forth by Fray Luis, and this christology,
focused on the Incarnation as the pinnacle of God's self-disclosure, was at the center of his understanding of revelation. It
also provided the core of his devotion to the interpretation
of the Bible and of his commitment to making this precious
divine gift available to ordinary people in their own Spanish
vernacular. For the eloquent and prolific Augustinian, Christ
was understood as "the key which unlocks the whole mystery
of human existence and the mystery of the universe. He is the
final and greatest act of God's communication of [*divine*] glory
to [*God's*] creation, and the hypostatic union reveals the destiny
which awaits every creature."[122]

[119] Thompson, *The Strife of Tongues*, 113.
[120] As Noreña affirms, "Both in his scholastic treatise *De Incarnatione*
and in the first chapter of *De los Nombres de Cristo* . . . Fray Luis defended with
extraordinary eloquence and vigor Scotus' opinion that the Incarnation of the
Son of God had been decreed by God before and independently from the fore-
knowledge of Adam's fall" (*Studies in Spanish Renaissance Thought*, 161).
[121] Thompson, *The Strife of Tongues*, 175.
[122] Thompson, *The Strife of Tongues*, 176.

A turn to the words of Fray Luis himself, in his treatment of "Bud," the first of the names of Christ that he considers in book one of *The Names of Christ*, makes all this eminently clear. It matters a great deal that Fray Luis set forth this understanding of the Incarnation not in the academic Latin of his treatise *De Incarnatione*, but in the accessibly elegant Spanish that was intended for a more popular readership. Marcelo addresses Sabino,

> I ask you if the end for which God created all things was only to communicate [*God*]self to them and if this gift and communication occurs in different ways and if some of these ways are more perfect than others. Does not reason seem to assume that such a great Creator, in such a great work, had as purpose to establish the largest and most perfect communication that was possible?[123]

When Sabino goes along with this, Marcelo proceeds,

> And the greatest . . . of those that are made and can be made is the personal union that is produced between the divine Word and the human nature of Christ, by which God became one with [*humankind*].[124]

Further affirmation from Sabino then leads Marcelo to affirm the necessity that

> God in order to produce this blessed and marvelous union created everything that is seen and unseen. The end for which everything was created, all the variety and beauty of the world, was to bring forth this mixture of God and humankind or the one who is both [*divine and human*]: Jesus Christ.[125]

---

[123] Fray Luis de León, *The Names of Christ*, 60.
[124] Fray Luis de León, *The Names of Christ*, 60.
[125] Fray Luis de León, *The Names of Christ*, 60.

These lines from *The Names of Christ* take us back to Burgaleta's observations about the influence of Ignatian spirituality on Acosta's *Historia*, his argument that the structure of the early Jesuit's work reflected the *contemplatio ad amorem* of the Spiritual Exercises in which the retreatant was invited to contemplate the presence of God in all of creation, in the whole ladder of being. For the Augustinian scholar and mystic, that ladder did not culminate with the human world, but with the Incarnation of the Word, God's ultimate masterwork. Yet for Fray Luis, the marvel of the Incarnation was the accessibility that it implied, the ongoing availability of divine self-disclosure in the Word of God in the Scriptures. From the perspective that Fray Luis offered, *Plura fecit Deus*, the awe-imbued contemplation of the manifold wonders of God's creation, is intimately conjoined with *Verbum caro factum est*, precisely because he so deeply appreciated the Incarnation of the Word as the culmination of God's actions.

While, unfortunately, we know precious little about the Spanish visitors who left these phrases behind when they visited Cave 18 on Mona Island, and while we can certainly not map even the most indirect of lines between them and Fray Luis, we can affirm—even if only modestly—that such language was not completely out of synch with important currents in sixteenth-century Spanish thought. This retrieval of a key voice from sixteenth-century Spain, taken together with considerations of the *encuentro* between Taíno and Spanish vernaculars thousands of miles away on an island betwixt-and-between Hispaniola and Puerto Rico, sets the stage for the attention that the next chapters in this study devote to twentieth- and twenty-first-century *encuentros* with indigenous inhabitants of the Americas.

CHAPTER 3

From the Amazon to the Tiber

Words Incarnate in the World

The first chapter of this book took us on a westward journey from Spain to Mona Island to chart the unusual encounter between two worldviews in the dark recesses of a cave, an encounter that led the European visitors to affirm *plura fecit Deus* and to think more broadly about the implications of John 1:14, *Verbum caro factum est*, even as at least one visitor was troubled enough to write *Dios te perdone* as a response to the images that were inscribed there in the Taíno vernacular. The quest for a hermeneutics both nuanced and supple enough to account for the two Latin inscriptions in Cave 18 then led us eastward across the Atlantic back from sixteenth-century Mona Island to sixteenth-century Spain. There we worked to retrieve elements of a hermeneutics of the vernacular that emerged from the distinctive set of opportunities and challenges involved in biblical translation during the *Siglo de Oro*. We saw how the figure of Fray Luis de León stands out in what Colin P. Thompson called the "Strife of Tongues." This chapter moves through time from the sixteenth century to the twenty-first in order to ask what difference this twofold retrieval might make for a disruptive cartographer who would chart a course for a Christian theology of revelation for the present day. We begin on the banks of the Tiber.

Dios Te Perdone

On Monday, October 21, 2019, a video surfaced on YouTube with the title, "Pachamama idols thrown into the Tiber river!" As the four-minute video begins, in the early hours of the morning the camera walks the viewer into the Church of Santa Maria in Traspontina, a church on Rome's via della Conciliazione that is not far from Saint Peter's Basilica. Once inside, the camera focuses from across the nave on two chapels on the right side of the nave, where a man—seen from behind—enters and stoops down to pick up several objects. Exiting one of the chapels, he genuflects toward the main altar and leaves the church. We then see him walking away from the church carrying what are now clearly identifiable as several identical wooden carvings of a nude pregnant woman depicted in profile. Without showing his face, the camera follows him as he makes his way toward Castel Sant'Angelo with the carvings. When he reaches the middle of the Ponte Sant'Angelo, the bridge much-photographed by tourists with its statues of angels holding the instruments of the Passion, he places the five carvings on the marble balustrade and then both he and the person recording the video push the carvings into the Tiber one at a time. With that, the four-minute video, which has no spoken narration or closed captioning, comes to an end.[1]

In a subsequent YouTube video that was posted on November 4, 2019, two weeks after the incident took place, Alexander Tschugguel came forward to identify himself as the person who was responsible for removing the carvings from the church and tossing them into the Tiber, claiming "I followed very closely what was happening in Rome surrounding the Amazon Synod." He made his way from Vienna to Rome to find out for himself

---

[1] St. Boniface Institute, "Pachamama idols thrown into the Tiber River," October 21, 2019, YouTube video, 4:04, https://youtu.be/xoB_gjuZgf8.

what was going on. After visiting Santa Maria in Traspontina several times and asking questions of the volunteers there, he concluded, "after all the visits and everything I heard, for me it was totally clear. This is against the first commandment: 'I am the Lord your God. You shall not have other gods beside me. You shall not bow down to any graven image.' And then I saw them bowing down to this particularly graven image in the Vatican Gardens." Returning to Austria, he and some friends deliberated about what they should do, ultimately deciding, "We should get the statues out of church. They do not belong in a Catholic church."[2] So, he returned to Rome and took his place as a footnote in the history of the Amazonian Synod.

The story of these carvings is both much simpler and more complex than this curious and disturbing narrative suggests, bound up as this incident is with the multiple controversies that surrounded the Special Assembly of the Synod of Bishops for the Pan-Amazonian Region that took place in Rome from October 6 to 27, 2019. The event in the Vatican Gardens to which Tschugguel refers in the November 4 video is the prayer service that took place on October 4, the Feast of Saint Francis of Assisi, during which some of those who were in Rome for the Synod gathered to plant a tree, and during which Pope Francis consecrated the Synod to Saint Francis. The Vatican News report of this event began by pointing out that "the phrase 'Everything is connected' recurs often in Pope Francis' Encyclical, Laudato Si'," and that "During a unique ceremony in the Vatican Gardens on Friday, signs, symbols and songs, ensured that everything really

---

[2] St. Boniface Institute, "Why we threw the Pachamama idols into the Tiber river," November 4, 2019, YouTube video, 5:25, https://youtu.be/1p74CEA1_go. See Edward Pentin, "Austrian Catholic: Why I Threw Pachamama Statues into the Tiber," *National Catholic Register*, November 5, 2019, https://www.ncregister.com/blog/austrian-catholic-why-i-threw-pachamama-statues-into-the-tiber.

was 'connected.'" Organized by the Global Catholic Climate Movement, the Pan-Amazonian Ecclesial Network (REPAM),[3] and the Order of Friars Minor, the culmination of the event was the planting of an oak sapling from Assisi. Reflecting the holistic vision of *Laudato Si'*,

> Even the soil in which the tree was planted came steeped in significance. There was soil from the Amazon, celebrating the wealth of the bioregion's cultures and traditions; earth from India, representing countries most vulnerable to the climate crisis, where droughts and floods leave millions devastated; soil representing refugees and migrants, forced to leave their homes because of war, poverty, and ecological devastation. There was earth from places of human trafficking, and from sustainable development projects around the world. And there was more soil from the Amazon, earth bathed in the blood of those who have died fighting against its destruction.[4]

After the opening prayer, a Franciscan friar introduced an Amazonian delegation as they entered singing "*Remei, Remei*" ("I rowed, I rowed," the entrance hymn from the 2003 Amazonian *Missa Cabocla, uma Prece Amazônica*, by the Brazilian group Raízes Caboclas).[5] Dancing around a mandala, they

---

[3] Red Eclesial Panamazónica, https://redamazonica.org/identidad/.

[4] Vatican News, "Pope consecrates Synod for the Amazon to Saint Francis of Assisi," October 4, 2019, https://www.vaticannews.va/en/pope/news/2019-10/pope-synod-amazon-saint-francis-vatican-gardens.html?fbclid=IwAR0m_fYmz-Wd-b-mSqTc1RaNpUSaBeH8Gji05xM-7SH9CHV6LMlE3O5avYns. This includes a link to the video of the event.

[5] The lyrics can be found at: Banzeiro: The Amazon Climate Roller Coaster, http://banzeiro.greenarkpress.com/missa-cabocla-een-amazonegebed/. Thanks to Jonathan Y. Tan for this reference.

brought symbols of Amazonia, and remembrances of martyrs. The latter included a photo of Notre Dame de Namur Sister Dorothy Stang, who was assassinated in Brazil in 2005 because of her advocacy on behalf of Amazonian farmers.[6] The Amazonian delegation placed their symbols on a decorated cloth, bowing low in appropriate reverence, a matter of veneration and not of worship.

Several of the objects were then presented to Pope Francis, among them one of the wooden carvings that was later tossed into the Tiber. As an indigenous woman came to the pope carrying one of these, she bowed to him courteously and made the sign of the cross, as Pope Francis also did before the two of them shook hands. The image was identified aloud as "Our Lady of Amazonia." The pope then blessed it with the sign of the cross and received it. There could be no doubt in the mind of any reasonable observer about the indisputably and profoundly Christian character of what took place in the Vatican Gardens that day, and yet the distinctively Amazonian vernacular of the event was equally clear.[7] On that day the Amazon was flowing into the Tiber![8] As Rita Ferrone explained in an article that

---

[6] Barbara Fraser, "On feast of St. Francis, pope joins Amazonians to plant tree at Vatican," October 4, 2019, https://www.ncronline.org/news/feast-st-francis-pope-joins-amazonians-plant-tree-vatican

[7] Vatican News, "Tree planting ceremony in the Vatican Gardens," October 4, 2019, https://youtu.be/1wioisaIU2I.

[8] Variations of this phrasing appear as well in reference to the Synod of the Amazon by journalist Christopher Lamb. See Christopher Lamb, *The Outsider: Pope Francis and His Battle to Reform the Catholic Church* (Maryknoll, NY: Orbis Books, 2020), 170 ["For three weeks in Rome, the river of the Amazon flowed into the Tiber, bringing fresh water and evangelizing energy]; Pope Francis, *Beloved Amazonia: The Apostolic Exhortation and Other Documents*, with Introduction by Christopher Lamb (Maryknoll, NY: Orbis Books, 2020), viii ["Through the synod, the Amazon has flowed into the Tiber, seeking an Amazonian face for the church"].

appeared in *Commonweal*,

> No one in the delegation who set up the display, nor those in the organizing committee of the synod who had experience in the region, seemed at all ruffled by the presence of the images of the pregnant women. Pope Francis, who has a great respect for popular piety, was the least disturbed of all. He received the woman kindly, and gave his blessing to the image. When asked about the provenance of the figure, Fr. Fernando Lopez, SJ, an itinerant preacher who travels to the remote regions of the Amazon with a missionary group, said they had been using this image for years. They bought it in an artisan's market in Brazil.[9]

Bishop David Martínez, "who pointed out that he had seen this image on other occasions," explained, "We all have different interpretations: the Virgin Mary, Mother Earth . . . women, fertility, life; Amazonia is meant to be full of life."[10] Despite such reassurances that the image was no idol, Alexander Tschugguel took the images from Santa Maria in Traspontina and unceremoniously threw them into the Tiber, an act that gained him notoriety in some quarters and considerable praise in others. The November 4 YouTube video documenting the theft garnered comments that included "God will not be mocked. *Christus vincit!*" "Well done! I'm glad someone had the courage to remove these

---

[9] Rita Ferrone, "A Hermeneutic of Suspicion: Pope Francis's Critics & the Amazon Statues," *Commonweal*, November 4, 2019, https://www.commonwealmagazine.org/hermeneutic-suspicion. For a first-hand perception of the ceremonies and the Synod and an analysis of the aftermath see journalist Christopher Lamb, "Introduction," in *Beloved Amazonia: The Apostolic Exhortation and Other Documents* and his "Epilogue" in *The Outsider*.

[10] Ferrone, "A Hermeneutic of Suspicion."

evil idols from the church. This must be an awakening for Pope Francis: the faithful will not tolerate this evil in his church," as well as "As a brazilian [*sic*]: May Our Lord Jesus Christ bless you people from taking the evil out of our church. My country is heretic to its very foundations, and you should reject vehemently pretty much everything that comes from here. *Ave Christus Rex!*"

On October 21, at the beginning of the afternoon session of the Synod, Pope Francis himself apologized for the theft of the images, asking pardon of anyone who was offended by the theft and by their being thrown into the Tiber. The pope also reported that the images had been recovered by the Italian authorities.[11] His impromptu remarks included the following:

> Good afternoon, I would like to say a word about the pachamama statues that were removed from the Church at Traspontina, which were there without idolatrous intentions and were thrown into the Tiber. First of all, this happened in Rome and, as bishop of the diocese, I ask pardon of the people who were offended by this act. Then, I can inform you that the statues which created so much media clamor were found in the Tiber. The statues are not damaged.[12]

These remarks infuriated critics of Pope Francis and of the Amazonian Synod, particularly his casual—and inaccurate—refer-

---

[11] See John L. Allen, "Pope apologizes for theft of Pachamama, says she could be back Sunday," *Crux*, October 25, 2019, https://cruxnow.com/amazon-synod/2019/10/pope-apologizes-for-theft-of-pachamama-says-shell-be-back-on-sunday/.

[12] As quoted in Edward Pentin, "Pope Francis' Words Announcing Pachamama Recovery," *National Catholic Register*, October 25, 2019, https://www.ncregister.com/blog/pope-francis-words-announcing-pachamama-recovery.

ence to the images as "pachamama statues," even leading *Benedict Option* author Rod Dreher to dub him "the Pachamama Pope."[13] On October 26, 2019, the day after the pope's apology, Father David Nix, who goes by "The Pilgrim Priest" on his blog, shared the following with his readers: "I spent the last week in Rome to make reparation for the Amazon Synod. I am not one of the men who dunked the pagan idols into the Tiber, but I wish I had been one of them." He added, "When I was making a Holy Hour of reparation in Santa Maria of Transpontina this week, it hit me that the pagan idols were just the outgrowth of Catholics accepting 100 years of ecumenism."[14] Even worse than the rantings of the likes of Dreher or of "pilgrim priest" was the October 24, 2019 appearance of Cardinal Gerhard Müller, former prefect of the Congregation of the Doctrine of the Faith, on EWTN's *The World Over Live*, where he claimed that bringing the "idols" into the church was a grave sin and a crime against divine law, even though those who were responsible for throwing them into the Tiber may have violated human law.[15] Perhaps still worse were the words of praise that Cardinal Raymond

---

[13] Rod Dreher, "The Pachamama Pope," *The American Conservative*, October 26, 2019, https://www.theamericanconservative.com/dreher/the-pachamama-pope/?fbclid=IwAR3-ESIlrnqGfqgdsZsaPiEp-5c6otWeInwwNyIkWNVaFL6MAVoG5oeaL3f8. See idem, *The Benedict Option: A Strategy for Christians in a Post-Christian Nation* (New York: Sentinel, 2017).

[14] David Nix, The Pilgrim Priest, October 26, 2019, https://padreperegrino.org/2019/10/amazonsynod/.

[15] Maike Hickson, "Cardinal Müller: 'The great mistake was to bring the idols into the Church, not to put them out,'" Lifesite News, October 24, 2019, https://www.lifesitenews.com/news/cardinal-mueller-the-great-mistake-was-to-bring-the-idols-into-the-church-not-to-put-them-out. How curious it is that the very same Cardinal Müller co-authored a book with Gustavo Gutiérrez, and that he regularly spent extended periods of time in Latin America! See Gustavo Gutiérrez and Gerhard Ludwig Müller, *On the Side of the Poor: The Theology of Liberation*, trans. Robert A. Krieg and James B. Nickoloff (Maryknoll, NY: Orbis Books, 2015).

Burke had for Tschugguel toward the end of a November 9, 2019, *New York Times* interview with Ross Douthat. When asked about Tschugguel, Burke praised him for his pro-life activities, but quickly pivoted to tell Douthat, "I had nothing to do with his removal of the pagan idols from the Church of Santa Maria in Traspontina and his throwing them into the Tiber." Yet, without skipping a beat, Burke went on to say, "At the same time, knowing his deep Catholic faith, I can understand why he found it intolerable that pagan idols be displayed in a Catholic church"; he then went on to express his gratitude to Tschugguel "for his courageous witness to the faith."[16]

Several centuries earlier, an unnamed European visitor to Cave 18 on Mona Island wrote *"Dios te perdone"* in response to what he saw, in marked contrast to the Latin inscriptions left by his contemporaries that communicated a far different take on the Taíno pictographs that were made in that sacred space beyond the reach of sunlight. The intolerance of difference betrayed in the ease with which so many critics of the Amazonian Synod leveled the charge of idolatry, and the violence of words exacerbated by the willingness of some to toss misunderstood cultural artifacts into the Tiber, compounded by the applause that this crime against Amazonian indigenous culture garnered from more than a few, is painfully reminiscent of centuries-old intolerance that led to violence an ocean away when Europeans first landed in the Americas. *Dios te perdone*, then, perhaps is a phrase that echoes from sixteenth-century Mona Island to twenty-first-century Rome as a prayer uttered for the sake of such people as Alexander Tschugguel.

Contrition and Confession

---

[16] Ross Douthat, "Cardinal Burke: 'I'm Called the Enemy of the Pope, Which I Am Not:' A conversation with Cardinal Raymond Burke," *New York Times*, November 9, 2019. https://www.nytimes.com/2019/11/09/opinion/cardinal-burke-douthat.html.

While *Dios te perdone* was written by a European to invoke divine mercy on the Taínos in whose sacred space that visitor stood, beholding motifs and pictographs that held meaning in a vernacular the visitor did not understand, the other side of sin is repentance, contrition, and confession. These are the conditions for the possibility of authentic reconciliation. On July 9, 2015, during his first visit as bishop of Rome to the continent where he was born, Pope Francis addressed the following words to the participants in the Second World Meeting of Popular Movements, in Santa Cruz de la Sierra, Bolivia:

> Let us say no . . . to forms of colonialism old and new. Let us say yes to the encounter between peoples and cultures. Blessed are the peacemakers. Here I wish to bring up an important issue. Some may rightly say, "When the Pope speaks of colonialism, he overlooks certain actions of the Church." I say this to you with regret: many grave sins were committed against the native peoples of America in the name of God. My predecessors acknowledged this, CELAM, the Council of Latin American Bishops, has said it, and I too wish to say it. Like Saint John Paul II, I ask that the Church—I repeat what he said—"kneel before God and implore forgiveness for the past and present sins of her sons and daughters." I would also say, and here I wish to be quite clear, as was Saint John Paul II: I humbly ask forgiveness, not only for the offenses of the Church herself, but also for crimes committed against the native peoples during the so-called conquest of America. Together with this request for forgiveness and in order to be just, I also would like us to remember the thousands of priests and bishops who strongly opposed the logic of the sword with the power of the Cross. There was sin, a great

deal of it, for which we did not ask pardon. So for this, we ask forgiveness, I ask forgiveness.[17]

This confession is markedly different from the confession offered by his predecessor John Paul II, which Pope Francis mentions. In *Incarnationis Mysterium*, the bull of indiction for the Jubilee Year 2000, John Paul II wrote, "As the Successor of Peter, I ask that in this year of mercy the Church, strong in the holiness which she receives from her Lord, should kneel before God and implore forgiveness for the past and present sins of her sons and daughters."[18] While John Paul II asked that the whole Church should ask forgiveness *from God* for the sins committed by "her sons and daughters," without specifically naming any of these sins, Pope Francis went much further.[19] First of all, he spoke

---

[17] Pope Francis, Address at the Second World Meeting of Popular Movements, in Santa Cruz de la Sierra, Bolivia, July 9, 2015, http://www.vatican.va/content/francesco/en/speeches/2015/july/documents/papa-francesco_20150709_bolivia-movimenti-popolari.html.

[18] John Paul II, *Incarnationis Mysterium*, Bull of Indiction of the Great Jubilee Year of the Year 2000, November 29, 1998, https://www.vatican.va/jubilee_2000/docs/documents/hf_jp-ii_doc_30111998_bolla-jubilee_en.html

[19] In his opening address at the Fourth General Conference of CELAM in Santo Domingo in 1992, instead of asking pardon for the Church's sins committed in the midst of the "first steps of evangelization" in the Americas, Pope John Paul II emphasized instead the role of the Church as "a tireless defender of the Indians, a protector of the values present in their cultures and a promoter of humane treatment in the face of the abuses of sometime unscrupulous colonizers" (John Paul II, Opening Address on the Occasion of the 4th General Conference of the Latin American Episcopate, October 12, 1992, in *Santo Domingo and Beyond: Documents and Commentaries from the Fourth General Conference of Latin American Bishops*, ed. Alfred T. Hennelly [Maryknoll, NY: Orbis Books, 1993], 43). In his Message to the Indigenous communities of the American Continent, delivered on October 12, 1992, in Santo Domingo, John Paul II asked, "During this Fifth Centenary, how could the Church, which with its

not in general terms but specifically to those who were gathered in Bolivia, not to ask *them* to beg forgiveness but to "ask forgiveness, not only for the offenses of the Church herself, but also for crimes committed against the native peoples during the so-called conquest of America." The pope's mention of "the thousands of priests and bishops who strongly opposed the logic of the sword with the power of the Cross" did not avoid the honest acknowledgment of the sins to which he admitted, for he then repeated, "There was sin, a great deal of it, for which we did not ask pardon. So for this, we ask forgiveness, I ask forgiveness," including a long history of not asking pardon among the sins that he confessed.

What precedes and follows the papal confession for the crimes of the Church against indigenous peoples during the "so-called conquest of America," as Pope Francis referred to it, is also important. The "no" to colonialism—not merely as a historical artifact but also as a present reality ("which reduces poor countries to mere providers of raw material and cheap labor, engenders violence, poverty, forced migrations and all the evils which go hand in hand with these")—simultaneously involves a "yes" to "the encounter between peoples and cultures." Pope Francis elaborates on his vision for the configuration of that encounter in a paragraph of the same speech that follows not long after his confession:

> To our brothers and sisters in the Latin American indigenous movement, allow me to express my deep affection

---

religious, priests and bishops has always been at the side of the indigenous people, forget the enormous suffering inflicted on the inhabitants of this Continent during the time of conquest and colonization? We must truly acknowledge the abuses committed due to the lack of love of those people who did not know how to see in the indigenous their brothers and sisters and children of God the same Father" (https://www.vatican.va/content/john-paul-ii/es/messages/pont_messages/1992/documents/hf_jp-ii_mes_19921012_indigeni-america.html). Translation mine.

and appreciation for their efforts to bring peoples and cultures together—a coming together of peoples and cultures—in a form of coexistence which I like to call polyhedric, where each group preserves its own identity by building together a plurality which does not threaten but rather reinforces unity. Your quest for an interculturalism, which combines the defense of the rights of the native peoples with respect for the territorial integrity of states, is for all of us a source of enrichment and encouragement.[20]

This "polyhedric form of coexistence," as Pope Francis calls it, is a decisive step beyond the more conventional notion of inculturation, which has too often been misconstrued as a linear process that works only in one direction, with evangelization construed as a matter of pouring the same Gospel into a variety of colorfully crafted cultural containers.[21] Following the logic of that metaphor,

---

[20] Pope Francis, Address at the Second World Meeting of Popular Movements, in Santa Cruz de la Sierra, Bolivia, July 9, 2015, https://www.vatican.va/content/francesco/en/speeches/2015/july/documents/papa-francesco_20150709_bolivia-movimenti-popolari.html

[21] Pope John Paul II provided a brief definition of inculturation as "the incarnation of the Gospel in native cultures and also the introduction of these cultures into the life of the Church" (*Slavorum Apostoli*, No. 21, https://www.vatican.va/content/john-paul-ii/en/encyclicals/documents/hf_jp-ii_enc_19850602_slavorum-apostoli.html). In *Redemptoris Missio*, John Paul II elaborates on inculturation in his treatment of "Incarnating the Gospel in Peoples' Culture (*Redemptoris Missio*, No. 52-54, https://www.vatican.va/content/john-paul-ii/en/encyclicals/documents/hf_jp-ii_enc_07121990_redemptoris-missio.html). Also see Congregation for Divine Worship and the Discipline of the Sacraments, *The Roman Liturgy and Inculturation: Fourth Instruction for the Right Application of the Conciliar Constitution on the Liturgy* (Vatican City: Libreria Editrice Vaticana, 1994). Also see Néstor Medina, *Christianity, Empire, and the Spirit: (Re)Configuring Faith and the Cultural* (Leiden: Brill, 2018), especially 253–307, "Inculturation, the Catholic Church, and the Cultures of

the container has no impact on the substance, the consistency, the flavor, or even the temperature of the Gospel that has been poured into it.[22] The aim, according to this model, is accurate translation from the single source into a variety of target languages. Pope Francis proposes a different model of *encuentro*, one that is three-dimensional and that involves more than merely linear movement, not inculturation as it has typically been understood but interculturalism. This is not to be confused with multiculturalism, which is rightly criticized both as superficial and also as a thin veneer of admissible diversity that does little to disrupt or to unseat the dominant voices that retain control over what is at stake. A polyhedric approach to interculturality is neither two-dimensional nor linear, and the dialogue moves in as many directions as there are participants in the process, with each contributing from a position of strength while respecting what every participant brings to the table.[23]

---

the World." Also see Robert J. Schreiter, "Faith and Cultures: Challenges to a World Church," *Theological Studies* 50 (1989): esp. 753–760; as well as Cardinal Gianfranco Ravasi, "Prologue," in *The Word Became Culture*, ed. Miguel H. Díaz (Maryknoll, NY: Orbis Books, 2020), xxiii. Here Ravasi points to the description of inculturation in the May 1980 address of Pope John Paul II to the bishops of Kenya: "The 'acculturation' or 'inculturation' which you rightly promote will truly be a reflection of the Incarnation of the Word, when a culture, transformed and regenerated by the Gospel, brings forth from its own living tradition original expressions of Christian life, celebration and thought."

[22] In his treatment of the Second Vatican Council's Pastoral Constitution on the Church in the Modern World (*Gaudium et Spes*) Medina notes how the Council worked to maintain "the delicate balance between the integrity of the Gospel and safeguarding local cultural traditions and customs" (Medina, *Christianity, Empire, and the Spirit*, 277, referencing *Gaudium et Spes* 94).

[23] In an August 2019 interview with Domenico Agasso Jr., Pope Francis elaborated on this "polyhedric" approach. Answering a question about the importance of identities, he replied: "Let me give you the example

Both in his confession of the Church's sins and in his vision for a polyhedric model of the encounter of peoples and cultures, Pope Francis moves in a different direction from the approach outlined by his immediate predecessor Pope Benedict XVI in his address at the inaugural session of the Fifth General Conference of the Bishops of Latin America and the Caribbean (CELAM) at Aparecida, Brazil, in May 2007. As Archbishop of Buenos Aires, Pope Francis was present at Aparecida and heard this address himself. Benedict XVI asked, "What did the acceptance of the Christian faith mean for the nations of Latin America and the Caribbean?" He went on to answer:

> For them, it meant knowing and welcoming Christ, the unknown God whom their ancestors were seeking, without realizing it, in their rich religious traditions. Christ is the Saviour for whom they were silently longing. It also meant that they received, in the waters of Baptism, the divine life that made them children of God by adoption; moreover, they received the Holy Spirit who came to make their cultures fruitful, purifying them and devel-

---

of ecumenical dialogue: I can't do ecumenism if I don't start from my being Catholic, and the other who does ecumenism with me must do so as a Protestant, an Orthodox. . . . Our own identity is not negotiable, it integrates itself. The problem with exaggerations is that we isolate our own identity instead of open ourselves. Identity is a wealth—cultural, national, historical, artistic—and each country has its own, but it must be integrated with dialogue. This is crucial: starting from our own identity we must open to dialogue in order to receive something greater from the identity of others. Never forget that "the whole is greater than the parts." Globalization, unity, should not be conceived as a sphere, but as a polyhedron: each people retains its identity in unity with others" (Domenico Agasso Jr., "Pope Francis warns against sovereignism: 'It leads to war,'" *La Stampa*, August 9, 2019, https://www.lastampa.it/vatican-insider/en/2019/08/09/news/pope-francis-warns-against-sovereignism-it-leads-to-war-1.37330049/).

oping the numerous seeds that the incarnate Word had planted in them, thereby guiding them along the paths of the Gospel. In effect, the proclamation of Jesus and of his Gospel did not at any point involve an alienation of the pre-Columbian cultures, nor was it the imposition of a foreign culture.[24]

This characterization of the beginnings of Christianity in Latin America met with loud protest from indigenous peoples. According to a *Los Angeles Times* story, "Indigenous groups from Chile to Mexico have condemned the remarks as a revision of a history marked by massacres, enslavement and destruction of native cultures."[25] One Quechua group commented, "Surely the pope doesn't realize that the representatives of the Catholic Church of that era, with honorable exceptions, were complicit, accessories and beneficiaries of one of the more horrible geno-cides that humanity has seen," while "A Peru-based alliance of Andean Indians, in an open letter to Benedict, wrote that the pope must know that 'the so-called evangelization was violent,' adding, 'Any cult that wasn't Catholic was persecuted and cruelly repressed.'"[26] The notion that the indigenous cultures of Latin America needed to be purified, together with the denial that missionary activities involved the alienation of those cultures or that it involved the imposition of a foreign culture also generated

---

[24] Benedict XVI, Address at the inaugural session of the Fifth General Conference of the Bishops of Latin America and the Caribbean, Aparecida, Brazil, May 13, 2007, https://www.vatican.va/content/benedict-xvi/en/speeches/2007/may/documents/hf_ben-xvi_spe_20070513_conference-aparecida.html

[25] Patrick J. McDonnell, "Latin American groups, leaders decry pope's remarks on conquest," *Los Angeles Times*, May 23, 2007, https://www.latimes.com/archives/la-xpm-2007-may-23-fg-pope23-story.html.

[26] McDonnell, "Latin American groups, leaders decry pope's remarks on conquest."

considerable opposition.

Perhaps in response to the controversy that his Aparecida address sparked, Pope Benedict returned to the topic in remarks at his May 23, 2007, general audience in St. Peter's Square, during which he reflected on his apostolic journey to Brazil earlier that month. He admitted,

> Certainly, the memory of a glorious past cannot ignore the shadows that accompany the work of evangelization of the Latin American Continent: it is not possible, in fact, to forget the suffering and the injustice inflicted by colonizers on the indigenous populations, whose fundamental human rights were often trampled upon. [27]

Still, Pope Benedict stopped short of issuing the sort of apology for these misdeeds on which the critics of his Aparecida address had insisted. He spoke of shadows that accompanied the work of evangelization, as though the process of evangelization itself was pure, untainted, and blameless, making it seem that the "suffering and the injustice inflicted by the colonizers on the indigenous populations" had nothing to do with the European missionary efforts that were integral to the process of colonization. Further, Pope Benedict suggested that

> the obligation to recall such unjustifiable crimes—crimes, however, already condemned at the time by missionaries like Bartolomé de Las Casas and by theologians like Francisco de Vitoria of the University of Salamanca—must not prevent noting with gratitude the wonderful works accomplished by divine grace among those populations in

---

[27] Benedict XVI, General Audience, May 23, 2007, http://www.vatican.va/content/benedict-xvi/en/audiences/2007/documents/hf_ben-xvi_aud_20070523.html.

the course of these centuries.[28]

This "accentuate the positive" twist also proved profoundly unsatisfying, coupled as it was with his affirmation of the Catholic identity of what he called "the Latin American people" as "the most adequate response" to the present age of globalization and its challenges. Perhaps it was his own memory of his predecessor's Aparecida address and its shortcomings that motivated—at least in part—Pope Francis's apology for the sins of the Church during his own first visit back to his native Latin America and his articulation of a polyhedric model of intercultural *encuentro*. Perhaps the lingering memory of his predecessor's *faux pas* on Latin American soil was one among the many factors that led to the Amazonian Synod. Clearly, the Amazonian Synod struck a sensitive nerve in some quarters that recognized how deeply such a gathering, convened during the pontificate of the first Latin American bishop of Rome, challenged a solidly entrenched Eurocentric vision of what it means to be Catholic in the twenty-first century. For a change, the Amazon was flowing into the Tiber: consider that chapter one of the Synod's final document begins by quoting Revelation 22:1, "Then the angel showed me the river of life-giving water, sparkling like crystal, flowing from the throne of God and of the Lamb."

Seeds of the Word in Amazonia

In reading the Final Document of the Amazonian Synod, it is not long before we find the first reference to indigenous practices, attitudes, and values framed in markedly positive terms. The document identifies *buen vivir*, good living, as "a matter of living in

---

[28] Benedict XVI, General Audience, May 23, 2007, http://www.vatican.va/content/benedict-xvi/en/audiences/2007/documents/hf_ben-xvi_aud_20070523.html.

harmony with oneself, with nature, with human beings and with the Supreme Being," and it is here that we find mention—albeit indirect—of revelation, because this harmony exists "since there is intercommunication throughout the cosmos." This means that *buen vivir* "is characterized by the interconnection and harmony of relationships between water, territory and nature, community life and culture, God and various spiritual forces."[29]

There is nothing really new about this, because the Christian understanding of natural revelation, divine self-disclosure through creation itself, is as ancient as Romans 1:18–20: "For God's wrath is being revealed from heaven against all the godlessness and wickedness of human beings who by such wickedness stifle the truth: that what can be known about God is manifest to them. For God himself has made it evident for them. Ever since the creation of the world his invisible qualities, his eternal power and divinity, have been perceived by reflection on what he has made."[30] Paul's presentation in Romans echoes the argument of Wisdom 13:1, "all people who were ignorant of God were foolish by nature; and they were unable from the good things that are seen to know the one who exists, nor did they recognize the artisan while paying heed to his works," as well as Wisdom 13:5, "from the greatness and beauty of created things comes a corresponding perception of their Creator" (*NRSV*).[31] The second chapter of the First Vatican Council's Dogmatic Constitution on the Catholic Faith (*Dei Filius*),

---

[29] Special Assembly of the Synod of Bishops for the Pan-Amazon Region, *Final Document: The Amazon: New Paths for the Church and for an Integral Ecology*, October 26, 2019, https://www.vatican.va/roman_curia/synod/documents/rc_synod_doc_20191026_sinodo-amazzonia_en.html Subsequent references to this document will appear parenthetically in the text as *Amazon Synod Final Document*.

[30] The translation is from Joseph A. Fitzmyer, *Romans: A New Translation with Introduction and Commentary*, Anchor Bible 33 (New York: Doubleday, 1992), 269.

[31] See Fitzmyer, *Romans*, 272.

focusing on Revelation, begins by citing Romans 1:20 in support of its affirmation that the Church "holds and teaches that God, the beginning and end of all things, can be known with certainty from the things that were created through the natural light of human reason," and, further, "It is to be ascribed to this divine revelation that such truths among things divine, can, even in the present condition of [*human*]kind, be known to everyone with facility, with firm certitude, and with no admixture of error."[32]

The Second Vatican Council's Dogmatic Constitution on Divine Revelation (*Dei Verbum*) also cites Romans 1:19–20 early in the treatment of revelation itself in chapter one: "God, who through the Word creates all things (see John 1:3) and keeps them in existence, gives [*people*] an enduring witness to Himself in created realities (see Rom. 1:19–20)" (*Dei Verbum*, No. 3).[33] With the reference to John 1:3, this way of addressing divine self-disclosure in the work of creation frames it in a specifically christological key: "All things came into being through him [*the Word*], and without him not one thing came into being" (*NRSV*). Creation and revelation are not to be understood as two discrete and discon-

---

[32] Heinrich Denzinger, *Compendium of Creeds, Definitions, and Declarations on Matters of Faith and Morals*, revised, enlarged, and, in collaboration with Helmut Hoping, ed. Peter Hünermann, Robert Fastiggi, and Anne Englund Nash (43d edition; San Francisco: Ignatius Press, 2012), 3004–3005 (hereafter Denzinger-Hünermann): "Eadem sancta mater Ecclesia tenet et docet, Deum, rerum omnium principium et finem, naturali humanae rationis lumine e rebus creatis certo cognosci posse. . . . Huic divinae revelationi tribuendum quidem est, ut ea, quae in rebus divinis humanaerationi per se impervia non sunt, in praesenti quoque generis humani condicione ab omnibus expedite, firma certitudine et nullo admixto errore cognosci possint." In support of this position, *Dei Filius* also refers to Thomas Aquinas, *Summa theologiae* I, q 1, a 1.

[33] Denzinger-Hünermann 4202: "Deus per Verbum omnia creans (cf. Io 1:3) et conservans, in rebus creatis perenne sui testimonium hominibus praebet (cf. Rm 1:19s)."

nected acts—or sets of acts—on God's part. They are instead closely intertwined aspects of divine engagement with humankind. It is no surprise, therefore, that Pope Francis cites both Romans 1:20 and Wisdom 13:5 in *Laudato Si'*, in support of his affirmation that "Saint Francis, faithful to Scripture, invites us to see nature as a magnificent book in which God speaks to us and grants us a glimpse of his infinite beauty and goodness."[34] Pope Francis returns to the theme of creation *as revelation* later on in *Laudato Si'*. In the collegial style that has become something of a trademark practice for documents that bear his signature, in *Laudato Si'* Pope Francis weaves together insights from a 2003 pastoral letter of the Social Affairs Commission of the Canadian Conference of Catholic Bishops, and a message from the Catholic Bishops' Conference of Japan from 2000, as well as two quotations from John Paul II. He writes that

> God has written a precious book, "whose letters are the multitude of created things present in the universe." The Canadian bishops rightly pointed out that no creature is excluded from this manifestation of God: "From panoramic vistas to the tiniest living form, nature is a constant source of wonder and awe. It is also a continuing revelation of the divine." The bishops of Japan, for their part, made a thought-provoking observation: "To sense each creature singing the hymn of its existence is to live joyfully in God's love and hope." This contemplation of creation allows us to discover in each thing a teaching which God wishes to hand on to us, since "for the believer,

---

[34] Pope Francis, *Encyclical Letter Laudato Si' on Care for Our Common Home*, May 24, 2015, 12, https://www.vatican.va/content/francesco/en/encyclicals/documents/papa-francesco_20150524_enciclica-laudato-si.html. Subsequent references to this document will appear parenthetically in the text as *Laudato Si'*.

to contemplate creation is to hear a message, to listen to a paradoxical and silent voice." We can say that "alongside revelation properly so-called, contained in sacred Scripture, there is a divine manifestation in the blaze of the sun and the fall of night." (*Laudato Si'*, No. 85)

The only two instances of the word "revelation" found in *Laudato Si'* appear in this splendid paragraph, where creation is described as a three-dimensional polyphonic book to be contemplated with a sense of wonder and awe that transcends mere words because the book of creation was written and continues to be written by the *Logos*, who is God's own Word. The words of John Paul II quoted in this paragraph, the "paradoxical and silent voice" to which we are invited to listen, are inspired by the first verses of Psalm 19, a psalm in two parts that begins with God's praise in creation (verses 1–6) and ends with praise of the Torah (verses 7–14).[35] The psalmist sings, "The heavens are telling the glory of God. . . . There is no speech, nor are there words; their voice is not heard, yet their voice goes out through all the earth, and their words to the end of the world" (Psalm 19:1, 3–4 *NRSV*). The two parts of the psalm are complementary, offering praise for God's eloquent work in creation as well as the divine eloquence revealed in the Torah.

Thus, the harmony of relationships about which the Synod's Final Document speaks, a stance that characterizes *buen vivir* as "the search of the Amazonian indigenous peoples for life in its abundance" (No. 9), is a matter of responding responsibly in fidelity to the divine self-disclosure that is offered in the book of creation. The Final Document picks up this thread a bit later when it says that "The life of the Amazonian communities not

---

[35] John Paul II, General Audience, January 26, 2000, http://www.vatican.va/content/john-paul-ii/en/audiences/2000/documents/hf_jp-ii_aud_20000126.html.

yet under the influence of Western civilization is reflected in their beliefs and their rites regarding the spirits of the divinity, named in innumerable ways, active with and in the territory, with and in relation to nature" (No. 14). The document goes on to recognize how the indigenous peoples of Amazonia have been caring for God's creation for thousands of years, and then to insist that "The new paths of evangelization must be developed in dialogue with these fundamental wisdoms making themselves manifest as seeds of the Word" (No. 14). Here the Final Document speaks specifically of the beliefs and rites of indigenous communities that are "not yet under the influence of Western civilization" and *not* of inculturated indigenous Christian communities. It then proposes a rethinking of evangelization that involves the genuine mutuality of dialogue and that identifies the wisdom of these indigenous communities as "seeds of the Word."

We will circle back to consider in detail what the Final Document means by "seeds of the Word," an expression that we have already seen in the Aparecida address of Benedict XVI. In the Final Document, there is no mention of any need to "purify" the indigenous cultures, as there was in Pope Benedict's address. Engagement with the "seeds of the word" in the mapping of new paths for evangelization is a matter of dialogue with the wisdom of Amazonia's indigenous communities.

Before moving in that direction, it is worth pausing to consider how the Synod's Final Document reckons with the non-innocent history of the evangelization of Amazonia. In the paragraph that follows immediately after insisting on a path to evangelization that involves dialogue with the "fundamental wisdoms" of the indigenous peoples of Amazonia, the Final Document confesses that "The proclamation of Christ often took place in collusion with the powers that exploited the resources and oppressed the local populations" (No. 15). Because that simple admission of past sins would be hollow if not accompanied by a commitment to emendation in the present, the Final Document goes on to recognize that "the Church has the historic opportunity to distance itself from the new colonizing powers by listening to the Amazonian peoples and acting in a transparent and prophetic manner" (No. 15). Instead of conveniently relegating the sins of colonialism to an unfortunate and embarrassing past, the Synod's Final Document recognized not only the centuries-old scars that it left behind; it also acknowledged the ways in which colonialism has by no means disappeared. Tragically, it keeps resurfacing in myriad exploitative and extractive practices and policies that are continuing to operate ever more efficiently throughout Amazonia, damaging the environment and harming its population.

Seeds of the Word: Amazonian Synod 2019

The expression "seeds of the Word" occurs four times in the Final Document. In the first mention it characterizes the fundamental wisdoms of the indigenous peoples of Amazonia that need to be taken into account in projecting new paths for evangelization (*Amazon Synod Final Document*, No. 14). Each subsequent reference is quite important in the development of the Synod's overall theme, new paths for the church and for an integral ecology. In calling attention to "the cultural values of the Amazon's peoples," the Final Document affirms that

> The people of the Amazon possess teachings for life. The original peoples and those who arrived later and forged their identity in coexistence with them, bear cultural values in which we discover the seeds of the Word. In the jungle, not only is the vegetation intertwined between one species and another, but the peoples also interrelate among themselves in a network of alliances that enriches all. The jungle thrives from interrelations and interdependencies, and this happens in all areas of life. Thanks to this, the

Amazon's fragile equilibrium has endured for centuries. (*Amazon Synod Final Document*, 43)

The "teachings for life," the "cultural values" of the peoples of Amazonia are recognized as keys to *buen vivir* in the present and not as irrelevant relics of the precolonial past. These offer not only a path toward coexistence among peoples, but a holistic network of interrelationships that includes the natural world and that promotes the flourishing of all. In effect, the metaphor itself, "seeds of the Word," helps to highlight how closely nature and culture are intertwined, with each impacting the other in vital ways. If it is true that the cultural values of the peoples of Amazonia have made it possible to maintain the Amazon's fragile equilibrium for centuries, it is also true that "the deterioration of nature is closely connected to the culture which shapes human coexistence," as Pope Benedict XVI warned in his 2009 encyclical *Caritas in Veritate*, which was quoted by Pope Francis in *Laudato Si'* No. 6.[36] The Synod's Final Document goes on to praise the holistic orientation of the fundamental wisdom of Amazonia's peoples, asserting that the integrated vision they offer provides a welcome alternative to a tendency toward fragmentation that is so predominant: "The pattern of thinking of indigenous peoples offers an integrated vision of reality, capable of understanding the multiple connections existing throughout creation. This contrasts with the dominant current of Western thought that tends to fragment reality in order to understand it but then fails to articulate the relationships between the various fields of knowledge" (*Amazon Synod Final Document*, No. 44). While the Final Document does not invoke revelation *per se*, the use of the expression "seeds of the Word" makes it clear that

---

[36] Pope Benedict XVI, Encyclical Letter *Caritas in Veritate* on Integral Human Development in Charity and Truth, June 29, 2009, 51, http://www.vatican.va/content/benedict-xvi/en/encyclicals/documents/hf_ben-xvi_enc_20090629_caritas-in-veritate.html.

the Word through whom all things came to being is the ultimate source of the indigenous "teachings for life" and "cultural values."

The Final Document's next mention of "seeds of the Word" comes in a section on paths to an inculturated Church that focuses on the mystery of faith as reflected in an inculturated theology:

> So-called Indian theology, theology with an Amazonian face, and popular piety are already riches of the indigenous world, its culture and spirituality. When the missionary and pastoral agent brings the word of the Gospel of Jesus, there is a personal identification with the culture, and an encounter takes place from which are born witnessing, service, proclamation and the learning of languages. The indigenous world enriches the intercultural encounter with its myths, narrative, rites, songs, dance and spiritual expressions. (No. 54)

"Indian theology," *teología india*, which the Synod's Final Document identifies as "theology with an Amazonian face," refers to a broad current of indigenous theologies in Latin America that, as Juan F. Gorski has described it, is "based on the rediscovery, the appropriation, and assessment of the religious and cultural experiences and expressions of the original peoples of the Americas."[37] In 2011, Felipe Arizmendi Esquivel (then successor of Samuel Ruiz as bishop of San Cristóbal de las Casas and subsequently bishop-emeritus and cardinal), wrote of *teología India* that it is "unknown by some, misunderstood and attacked by others." Arizmendi mentions that while there had been some discussion of mentioning it by name in the Aparecida

---

[37] Juan F. Gorski, "El desarrollo histórico de la 'Teología India' y su aporte a la inculturación del Evangelio," in Pablo Suess, Juan F. Gosrki, Beat Dietschy, Fernando Mires, and José Luis Gómez-Martínez, *Desarrollo Histórico de la Teología India* (Iglesia, Pueblos y Cultura, 48–49; Quito, Ecuador: Ediciones Abya-Yala, 1998), 10.

Final Document in 2007, the proposal did not receive enough votes to pass.[38]

In the *encuentro* between the missionary and pastoral agent with indigenous peoples, each brings something of value to share. Missionaries and pastoral agents arrive with "a personal identification with the culture," and willingness to learn languages, the local vernaculars of their dialogue partners, while these partners bring to their intercultural encounters their *teología india* together with the "myths, narrative, rites, songs, dance and spiritual expressions" that are the starting points for this theology in Amazonian vernaculars. Here the Synod's Final Document recalls the statement found in the Concluding Document of CELAM's 1979 Third General Conference at Puebla, which emphasized that "cultures are not empty ground, devoid of authentic values. The evangelization of the Church is not a process of destruction, but of consolidation and strengthening of these values; a contribution to the growth of the 'seeds of the Word' present in various cultures" (as cited in *Amazon Synod Final Document*, No. 54). This is unmistakably aimed at missionaries and pastoral agents in the hope that they will not repeat the mistakes of the past.

The explicit mention of "So-called Indian theology, theology with an Amazonian face" suggests that indigenous participants in the *encuentro* bring not only what could be dismissed far too easily as unsophisticated "myths, narrative, rites, songs, dance and spiritual expressions," but also carefully considered theologies that are incarnate in local lived daily experience and that find expression in a broad range of indigenous vernaculars. While nothing further is said about *teología India* in the Final Document, its inclusion reflects the concern expressed in the suggestions offered by the

---

[38] Felipe Arizmendi Esquivel, "Perspectivas de la Teología India," CELAM, April 6, 2011, https://www.celam.org/Images/img_noticias/doc3 4d9e02c40c453_07042011_130pm.pdf

Synod's Working Document: "It is desirable to deepen existing Amazonian Indian theology, which will allow for a better and greater understanding of indigenous spirituality and thus avoid committing the historical errors that have violated many original cultures."[39] In particular, the Working Document called for the Synod "to take into account the original myths, traditions, symbols, knowledge, rites and celebrations that include transcendent, community and ecological dimensions."[40] Explicitly including *teología India* in the Synod's Final Document, however briefly, represents a significant step forward even beyond Aparecida, recognizing the appropriateness and the importance of local Christian theologies that are seriously engaged with the rich heritage and the present reality of indigenous peoples.

The fourth time the Synod's Final Document employs "seeds of the Word" is found in a section that traces "paths for an intercultural Church," under the heading of "respect for the cultures and rights of peoples." Here the Synod explicitly seeks to separate evangelization from its long and harmful association with colonialism:

> We are all invited to approach the Amazon peoples on an equal footing, respecting their history, their cultures, their style of "good living." Colonialism is the imposition of some people's ways of life on others, whether economically, culturally or religiously. We reject a colonial style of evangelization. Proclaiming the Good News of Jesus implies recognizing the seeds of the Word already present in cultures. The evangelization that we propose today for the Amazon is the inculturated proclamation that gener-

---

[39] Synod of Bishops, Special Assembly for the Pan Amazon, Working Document, The Amazon: New Paths for the Church and for Integral Ecology, June 2019, No. 98, http://secretariat.synod.va/content/sinodoamazonico/en/documents/pan-amazon-synod--the-working-document-for-the-synod-of-bishops.html.

[40] Special Assembly for the Pan Amazon, Working Document, No. 98.

ates intercultural processes, processes that promote the
life of the Church with an Amazonian face and identity.
(*Amazon Synod Final Document*, No. 55)

Recognizing that there is more to the insidious dynamics of
colonialism than territorial expansion alone, the Synod calls for an
approach to evangelization that does not enforce cultural supersessionism. As an encounter among equals, the proclamation of the
Gospel ought not to be a unilateral infusion of the evangelizers'
vernacular as normative. It should instead involve respect for Amazonian history, culture, and ways of life based on the recognition that
the "seeds of the Word" are evidence that God has been and continues
to be at work among the peoples of Amazonia. The proclamation of
the Gospel in Amazonia, the Synod insists, needs to be authentically
and not just superficially Amazonian, engaging intercultural processes
that do not involve any sort of erasure or ideological colonization.[41]

---

[41] Here the Synod's Final Document points to the opening remarks
offered by Pope Francis at the opening of the Synod's work: "let us also
approach the Amazonian peoples on tip-toe, respecting their history, their
cultures, their good way of living in the etymological sense of the word, not
in the social sense which we often attribute to them, because peoples have
a proper identity, all peoples have their wisdom, a self-awareness; peoples
have a way of feeling, a way of seeing reality, a history, a hermeneutic,
and they tend to be protagonists of their history with these matters, with
these qualities. And as outsiders we consider ideological colonizations that
destroy or diminish the characteristics of the peoples. Ideological colonization is very widespread. And without any entrepreneurial apprehension,
we consider offering them prepackaged programs, in order to 'discipline'
the Amazonian peoples, to discipline their history, their culture; or this
concern to 'domesticate' the indigenous peoples. When the Church has
forgotten this, that is, the way she should approach a people, she has not
been inculturated; she has actually come to disdain certain peoples. And
how many failures we regret today. Let us think of De Nobile in India,
of Ricci in China and so many others. The 'homogenizing and 'homogenative' centralism has not allowed the peoples' authenticity to emerge."
(Pope Francis, Opening of the Works of the Special Assembly of the

The Working Document prepared for the Amazonian Synod provides further clarity on the relationship between inculturation and interculturality, explaining that they are not contradictory but complementary:

> Just as Jesus became incarnate in a particular culture (inculturation), his missionary disciples follow in his footsteps. For this reason, Christians from one culture go out to meet people from other cultures (interculturality). This happened from the beginning of the Church when the Hebrew apostles brought the Good News to different cultures, such as Greek culture, discovering there "seeds of the Word." New paths of the Spirit emerged from that encounter and dialogue between cultures. Today, in the encounter and dialogue with cultures of the Amazon, the Church continues to search for new pathways.[42]

The Incarnation of the Word, the Synod's Working Document suggests, was *the* inculturation *par excellence.* Yet the particularity of that inculturation did not prevent the successful and effective translation of the Good News into other cultures, into other vernaculars. Those cultures, the Working Document makes clear, have never been empty boxes or blank slates, whether in first-century Greece or in twenty-first-century Amazonia.

Synod of Bishops for the Pan-Amazon Region on the Theme: "Amazonia: New Paths for the Church and for Integral Ecology, Greeting of Pope Francis," October 7, 2019, https://www.vatican.va/content/francesco/en/speeches/2019/october/documents/papa-francesco_20191007_apertura-sinodo.html)

[42] Synod of Bishops, Special Assembly for the Pan Amazon, Working Document, The Amazon: New Paths for the Church and for Integral Ecology, June 2019, No. 108, http://secretariat.synod.va/content/sinodoamazonico/en/documents/pan-amazon-synod--the-working-document-for-the-synod-of-bishops.html

CHAPTER 4

"Seeds of the Word"

A Latin American Cartography

The deep appreciation of indigenous Amazonian culture, values, religious beliefs and practices that the Amazonian Synod cast in explicitly incarnational terms as "seeds of the Word" did not emerge *ex nihilo* in Rome in October 2019, nor does the credit for this belong only to the Synod's Working Document. We can chart this increasingly positive evaluation of the role of indigenous cultures back through the General Conferences of CELAM from Aparecida in 2007, back to Santo Domingo in 1992, then back to Puebla in 1979, and to Medellín in 1968 where "seeds of the Word" was first used to provide an affirmative theological appreciation of indigenous Latin American cultures.

CELAM and the "Seeds of the Word"

Aparecida 2007

When "seeds of the Word" first appears in the Aparecida Concluding Document, the bishops explain how "The Gospel reached our lands as part of a dramatic and unequal encounter of peoples and cultures. The 'seeds of the Word,' present in the native cultures, made it easier for our indigenous brothers and

107

sisters to find in the Gospel life-giving responses to their deepest aspirations."[1] "Dramatic and unequal" is a serious understatement, to say the least, and the unspecified "seeds of the Word" are framed not as intrinsically valuable *per se* but as *praeparatio evangelica*, predisposing indigenous peoples of Latin America to receive the Gospel when it arrived from Europe. Not surprisingly, this first mention of seeds of the Word is accompanied by a quotation from Pope Benedict XVI's opening address, "Christ is the Savior for whom they were silently longing."[2]

The expression occurs a second time in the Aparecida Document, focusing on the presence of indigenous and Afro-American peoples in the Church, pointing back to the use of "seeds of the Word" in CELAM's 1992 Santo Domingo Concluding Document. The bishops note how at their Santo Domingo assembly they had "recognized that 'the indigenous peoples of today cherish very important human values;' values that 'the church defends . . . as they confront the overwhelming power of the structures of sin manifested in modern society,'" explaining further that these values are "bearers of a host of cultural riches that are the basis of our present culture," and that "from the standpoint of the faith, 'those values and convictions derive from "the seeds of the Word," which were already present at work in their ancestors'" (*Aparecida Document*, No. 92).

The Aparecida Document brings up "seeds of the Word" once again in its discussion of "indigenous and African-American" people, noting that "As disciples of Jesus Christ incarnate in the life of all peoples, with faith we discover and recognize the 'seeds of

---

[1] Fifth General Conference of Latin American and Caribbean Bishops, Final Document, Aparecida, Brazil, May 2007, No. 4, https://www.celam.org/aparecida/Ingles.pdf. Subsequent references to this document will appear parenthetically in the text as *Aparecida Document*.

[2] Benedict XVI, "Inaugural Address," Fifth General Conference of Latin American and Caribbean Bishops, May 13, 2007, No. 1, https://www.vatican.va/content/benedict-xvi/en/speeches/2007/may/documents/hf_ben-xvi_spe_20070513_conference-aparecida.html

the Word' present in the traditions and cultures of the indigenous peoples of Latin America" (No. 529).[3] The bishops elaborated on these, focusing on indigenous peoples' "deep communal appreciation for life, present in all creation, in everyday existence, and in the age-old religious experience which energizes their cultures," adding that this "reaches its fullness in the revelation of the true face of God by Jesus Christ" (*Aparecida Document*, No. 529). The bishops do not elaborate further on what they mean by referring to "age-old religious experience." However, in the face of efforts to erase indigenous identities and assimilate them, the bishops pledge to "accompany the indigenous and native peoples in strengthening their identities and their own organizations, the defense of their territory, bilingual intercultural education, and the defense of their rights" (*Aparecida Document*, No. 530).

At the same time, though, the bishops adopt what reads like a paternalistic and even infantilizing attitude towards the indigenous peoples of Latin America in what follows, cautioning that "The Church will remain vigilant in the face of efforts to uproot the Catholic faith from indigenous communities, whereby they would be left defenseless and confused in facing the assaults of the ideologies of some alienating groups, which would undermine the well-being of those very communities" (*Aparecida Document*, No. 531). The bishops do not specify what these threatening ideologies might be, nor do they identify the "alienating groups" that are seeking to advance them. Yet they argue that if the Catholic faith of Latin American indigenous communities were to be "uprooted" through the efforts of these "alienating groups," they would be left "defenseless and confused," and their well-being would be endangered. This attitude is concerning, especially if the indigenous peoples of Latin America are to be regarded as equal partners in

---

[3] In the English language translation of the Aparecida Document, No. 529 is numbered incorrectly as No. 528. See the original in Spanish https://www.celam.org/aparecida/Espanol.pdf.

dialogue. It might even seem as though the strengthening of identity to which the bishops are committed has more to do with Catholic identity than with the identities of indigenous people or the identities of people of African descent.

Santo Domingo 1992

Charting the path of "seeds of the Word" through the final documents of CELAM's general conferences take us next to Santo Domingo in 1992, the gathering that marked—for better or for worse—the fifth centenary of Columbus's first voyage in 1492. The bishops use "seeds of the Word" three times in the Final Document. In this document it first appears under the heading of "The Five Hundredth Anniversary of the First Evangelization," following shortly after a quotation from John Paul II's opening address in which he asserted that "In the peoples of the Americas, God has chosen for himself a new people whom he has . . . made sharers in his Spirit. Through evangelization and faith in Christ, God has renewed his covenant with Latin America."[4] This statement is highly significant of itself for three reasons. First, the language of election is important: the pope says that the peoples of the Americas are *chosen* by God. Second, the whole clause that follows reads, "*whom he has brought into his redemptive plan and* made sharers in his Spirit." The pope is affirming both that the peoples of the Americas are part of God's design and that God has bestowed the Spirit on them, yet he does not specify whether or not the gift of the Spirit occurred *prior* to the arrival of Europeans in the Americas.

---

    [4] Fourth General Conference of Latin American Bishops, Final Document: New Evangelization, Human Development, Christian Culture, Santo Domingo, October 1992, 16, as found in *Santo Domingo and Beyond: Documents and Commentaries from the Fourth General Conference of Latin American Bishops*, ed. Alfred T. Hennelly (Maryknoll, NY: Orbis Books, 1993), 77. Subsequent references to this document will appear parenthetically in the text as *Santo Domingo Document*.

Third—and this may offer a hint about what was suggested in the previous sentence—the pope clearly implies that it is an *already existing* covenant with the peoples of the Americas that was *renewed* "through evangelization and faith in Christ," and *not* that this covenant only came about when the missionaries arrived.[5] This is confirmed by John Paul II's quotation from his own January 1, 1992, homily that immediately precedes this remarkable sentence: "The peoples of the New World were 'new peoples . . . entirely unknown to the Old World until 1492,' but they were 'known to God from all eternity, and he had embraced them with the Fatherhood that the Son had revealed in the fullness of time.'"[6]

In what follows in the Santo Domingo concluding document, the Latin American bishops make it clear that their quotation from John Paul II's opening address represents more than a polite nod in the direction of the head of the college of bishops. They affirm that "God's creative, caring, and saving presence was already with these peoples. The 'seeds of the Word,' present in the deep religious sense of pre-Columbian cultures, was awaiting the fruitful sprinkling of the Spirit." What are these "seeds of the Word"? They go on to enumerate

> Along with other aspects that needed to be purified, these cultures at their core offered positive elements such as openness to God's action, the sense of gratitude for the fruits of the earth, the sacred character of human life and esteem for the family, the sense of solidarity and shared responsibility for work performed in common, the importance of worship, belief in a life beyond earth, and so many

[5] John Paul II, Opening Address on the Occasion of the 4th General Conference of the Latin American Episcopate, October 12, 1992, 3, in *Santo Domingo and Beyond*, 43.

[6] John Paul II, Opening Address on the Occasion of the 4th General Conference of the Latin American Episcopate, October 12, 1992, 3, in *Santo Domingo and Beyond*, 43.

other values that enrich the Latin American soul. (*Santo Domingo Document*, No. 17)

The bishops do not name any of the "aspects that need to be purified," and while the list of "positive elements" is lengthy, these are offered as examples of what is present in indigenous cultures "at their core." While the bishops suggest that these "seeds of the Word" were "awaiting the fruitful sprinkling of the Spirit" that—presumably— arrived on the shores of the Americas in 1492, the pope's opening address—from which they quote—by no means denies that the Spirit of God was active in the Americas prior to 1492. Quite the contrary!

The second of the three mentions of "seeds of the Word" in the Santo Domingo Document comes in its "Pastoral Directions" for "Engaging in Dialogue with Non-Christian Religions." There the bishops begin by highlighting "the importance of deepening a dialogue with the non-Christian religions on our continent, and especially with indigenous and African American religions, which have been ignored or shunted aside for a long time" (*Santo Domingo Document*, No. 137). After addressing the need to engage in dialogue with Jews and Muslims, the bishops go on to underscore the importance for interreligious dialogue of seeking "occasions for dialogue with African American and indigenous religions while being alert to discover in them 'seeds of the Word' with true Christian discernment, offering them the complete proclamation of the Gospel and avoiding any kind of religious syncretism" (*Santo Domingo Document*, No. 138). Here the task of discovering "seeds of the Word" in dialogue with "African American and indigenous religions" is strangely construed as a matter of dialogue with the religions themselves and not with the people who find meaning, value, and guidance in their practice of these ways of life. Rather than framing dialogue with people who are adherents of these religions as an opportunity for mutual enrichment, which would be the harvest of genuine dialogue, here such dialogue is framed in instrumental terms as a matter of the Catholic dialogue partner sifting the wheat from the chaff and identifying which is which "with true Christian discernment." At the same time, Catholic dialogue partners are instructed to "offer them the complete proclamation of the gospel," and by all means to "avoid any kind of religious syncretism," although what the former and the latter might involve is not further specified.

Mention of interreligious dialogue with Jews and Muslims as a pastoral priority is brief and somewhat benign, with the strange exception of the statement that these dialogues are worthwhile "despite the problems that the Church suffers in countries where these are the majority religions." The extreme caution the bishops express vis-à-vis interreligious dialogue with people who practice indigenous religions and religions of their African heritage seems defensive. Yet it is considerably less defensive than the following section of the document, devoted to what they call "The Fundamentalist Sects," and which begins with the statement that "The problem of the sects has reached dramatic proportions and has become truly worrisome, particularly due to increased proselytism" (*Santo Domingo Document*, No. 139). These "sects" are identified as "religious groups that insist that only faith in Jesus Christ saves, that the only basis for faith is Scripture interpreted personally in a fundamentalist manner, and hence excluding the Church; they emphasize the end of the world and the proximity of judgment" (*Santo Domingo Document*, No. 139).[7]

The third and final mention of "seeds of the Word" in the Santo Domingo document comes in chapter three, which deals with

---

[7] See Jean-Pierre Ruiz, "Naming the Other: U.S. Hispanic Catholics, the So-Called 'Sects,' and the 'New Evangelization,'" *Journal of Hispanic / Latino Theology* 4, no. 2 (November 1996): 34–59. Francisco Sampedro Nieto offers a very different perspective in "The Challenge of the Sects in Latin America," *Vincentiana* 42, no. 3 (1998), Article 7, https://via.library.depaul.edu/vincentiana/vol42/iss3/7.

Christian culture, and it appears under the heading of "Unity and Plurality of Indigenous, African American, and *Mestizo* Cultures,"[8] in the section that addresses "Pastoral Challenges." There the bishops begin by considering the multiethnic reality of Latin America and the Caribbean, where "indigenous, African American, and *mestizo* peoples and those descending from Europeans and Asians live together" (No. 244). They acknowledge that "while each group's own culture provides it with its own social identity in accord with each people's world vision, it is in their shared Catholic identity that unity is sought" (*Santo Domingo Document*, No. 244). The bishops then go on to name, in turn, the "pastoral challenges" that are faced in the Church's ministry with indigenous, African descendant, and *mestizo* populations. For each of the three groups, the bishops begin by identifying a few key features and then they consider specific pastoral challenges involving each of these sectors of the population.

With regard to the indigenous peoples of Latin America, the bishops recognize that they "cherish very important human values," a phrase that is quoted in the Aparecida document. The "seeds of the Word," they go on to say, are the source of these values, seeds "which were already at work in their ancestors, enabling them to go on to discover the Creator's presence in all his creatures: the sun, the moon, the earth, and so forth" (No. 245).[9] Pivoting then to identify

---

[8] In the Spanish original, this section is entitled "Unidad y pluralidad de las culturas indígenas, afroamericanas y mestizas."

[9] In the corresponding treatment of people of African descent, the bishops write that "African American cultures in Latin America and the Caribbean are marked by a continual resistance to slavery. These peoples, who number in the millions, also have in their cultures human values that express the presence of God the Creator" (*Santo Domingo Document*, No. 246). As for the corresponding sketch of key aspects, the *mestizo* population is a strange mixture of blessing and blame: "in those peoples that are the fruit of racial mixing, there has taken shape a particular *mestizo* culture in which popular religiosity, as an inculturated form of Catholicism, is very much alive. Nevertheless the failure to observe Christian obligations stands

pastoral challenges, the bishops paint an incomplete picture of the Church as an ally in the struggles of the indigenous peoples of the Americas that does not acknowledge the Church's complicity in the injustices committed against them. The bishops insist that "From its first encounters with these native peoples, the Church sought to accompany them as they struggled for survival out of the unjust situation of people who had been defeated, invaded, and treated as slaves, and it taught them the way of Christ the Savior." With a hefty measure of inappropriate pride that downplays the sin that was involved, they boast that "Along with enormous suffering, the first evangelization brought major accomplishments and attained valuable pastoral insights" (*Santo Domingo Document*, No. 245).

Stepping back to reflect on the use of "seeds of the Word" in the final documents that emerged from Aparecida and from Santo Domingo with an interest in what this suggests for a Christian theology of revelation, much more is implied here than the sort of natural revelation that can be traced back to Romans 1:18–20. What is affirmed by reference to "seeds of the Word" among the indigenous peoples of the Americas goes well beyond the affirmation of *Dei Filius* that God can be known through the natural light of human reason, and more also than the christological emphasis (from John 1:3) by which *Dei Verbum* frames divine self-disclosure in the work of creation. The bishops point to elements of indigenous culture, identified as "seeds of the Word." In the Santo Domingo document, for example, the bishops explain that these elements enable indigenous peoples to "go on to discover the Creator's presence in all his creatures," providing them with access to natural revelation (No. 245). Yet in the Santo Domingo Document (No.

---

side-by-side with admirable examples of Christian living, and ignorance of church teaching stands alongside Catholic experiences rooted in Gospel principles" (*Santo Domingo Document*, 247). It is noteworthy that only in their treatment of the *mestizo* population do the bishops point out shortcomings in their conduct.

17) the bishops also identified specific positive elements beyond what could be narrowly construed as divine self-disclosure through creation, among them "openness to God's action, the sense of gratitude for the fruits of the earth, the sacred character of human life and esteem for the family, the sense of solidarity and shared responsibility for work performed in common, the importance of worship, belief in a life beyond earth." At Aparecida and in Santo Domingo, the seeds of the word are understood to have been sown in indigenous traditions and cultures, reflecting the involvement of the Holy Spirit, activity that did not begin only with the arrival of Christianity that Europeans brought with them to the Americas in 1492.

Puebla 1979

In the final document that sums up CELAM's Third General Conference at Puebla in 1979, "seeds of the Word" appears in the context of a discussion about the Church, faith, and culture:

> In order to carry out its evangelizing activity realistically the Church must know the culture of Latin America. But, above all, it starts from a deep attitude of love towards peoples. In this way, not only by scientific means, but also by the innate capacity of affective understanding that love provides, it will be able to know and discern the modalities of our culture, its historical crises and its challenges and, consequently, to stand in solidarity with it at the heart of its history.[10]

It is important that the bishops prioritize familiarity with Latin American culture as a prerequisite for engagement in evan-

---

[10] Third General Conference of Latin American Bishops, Final Document, Puebla, México, May 1979, 397, http://www.celam.org/doc_conferencias/Documento_Conclusivo_Puebla.pdf. Translation mine. Subsequent references to this document will appear parenthetically in the text as *Puebla Document*.

gelization, and that this not only be a matter of academic expertise (*no sólo por vía científica*, not only by scientific means) but also through the sort of participatory insider knowledge that love makes possible. The bishops also recognize that culture is not static, and so they refer to the need to be aware of its "historical crises and challenges." It is equally important that they speak about Latin American culture as "our" culture, embracing their place as participants who stand in it in a position of participatory solidarity rather than as observers somehow standing outside of it. Yet to speak of Latin American *culture* in the singular is an overgeneralization that fails to acknowledge the broad range of Latin American *cultures* that exist, each with its own complex history and present reality.

The bishops then emphasize that, in becoming familiar with Latin American culture, it is more important to pay attention "to the general direction in which culture is moving than to enclaves that remain fixated on the past; more to current expressions than those that are merely folkloric" (*Puebla Document*, No. 398). This call for attention to present trends, coupled with the recognition that culture has a history (more accurately stated, cultures have histories), prevents attention to culture from becoming bogged down in nostalgia. Turning to what happens when Christian faith encounters culture, the bishops affirm, "When the Church, the People of God, announces the Gospel and the peoples receive the faith, it becomes incarnate in them and assumes their cultures. Thus, it [*the faith*] establishes, not an identification, but a close connection with it [*culture*]" (*Puebla Document*, No. 400). The language employed here emphasizes that faith becomes flesh in the particularity and the specificity of culture, Latin American culture in this case. Here the bishops affirm the pastoral relevance of the incarnational principle that they attribute to Irenaeus, "What is not assumed is not redeemed."[11]

---

[11] This oft-cited and oft-misquoted dictum, here misattributed to Irenaeus, actually comes from Gregory of Nazianzus, Letter 101 (to Cledonius

The Puebla Document quotes from the section of *Evangelii Nuntiandi* where Pope Paul VI explains the relationship between the Gospel and culture in these terms:

> The Gospel, and therefore evangelization, are certainly not identical with culture, and they are independent in regard to all cultures. Nevertheless, the kingdom which the Gospel proclaims is lived by men [*sic*] who are profoundly linked to a culture, and the building up of the kingdom cannot avoid borrowing the elements of human culture or cultures. Though independent of cultures, the Gospel and evangelization are not necessarily incompatible with them; rather they are capable of permeating them all without becoming subject to any one of them.[12]

Here Paul VI negotiates a delicate balance in describing the relationship between the Gospel and culture. While he asserts on the one hand that the Gospel cannot be swallowed up in culture and that it retains an autonomy that places it, in some sense, above culture, on the other hand the proclamation of the Gospel is inevitably bound up with culture. It would not be an exaggeration to say that, according to *Evangelii Nuntiandi*, the communication of the Gospel actually depends on culture, and not culture in general, but particular cultures, specific vernaculars.

---

the Presbyter), and it reads, "The unassumed is the unhealed, but what is united with God is also being saved." See St. Gregory of Nazianzus, *On God and Christ: The Five Theological Orations and Two Letters to Cledonius*, trans. Frederick Williams and Lionel Wickham (Crestwood, NY: St. Vladimir's Seminary Press, 2002), 158.

[12] Paul VI, Apostolic Exhortation *Evangelii Nuntiandi*, December 8, 1975, No. 20, https://www.vatican.va/content/paul-vi/en/apost_exhortations/documents/hf_p-vi_exh_19751208_evangelii-nuntiandi.html

The bishops' consideration of culture goes on to affirm that "Cultures are not empty terrain, devoid of authentic values. Evangelization by the Church is not a process of destruction, but of consolidation and strengthening of these values; a contribution to the growth of the 'seeds of the Word' present in cultures" (*Puebla Document*, No. 400). The "seeds of the word" are identified as "authentic values" that are already present in cultures prior to evangelization, and the process of evangelization ought not to uproot or eradicate them. Rather, it should "consolidate and strengthen" them. This is because these seeds, which provide the point of departure for evangelization, have been sown by Christ (*Puebla Document*, No. 403).[13] The process of evangelization, therefore, necessarily involves translation into the local cultural vernaculars: the Church—the particular Church—strives to adapt, making the effort to transfer the evangelical message to the human language (*lenguaje antropológico*] and symbols of the culture in which it is inserted" (*Puebla Document*, No. 404).

The bishops also make it clear that the Church does not simply embrace cultures uncritically whole and entire. Thus, when the Church presents the Good News, it

> denounces and corrects the presence of sin in cultures; purifies and exorcises what is not of value (*los desvalores*). It therefore establishes a critique of cultures. Since the other side of announcing the Kingdom of God is the critique of idolatries, that is, of the values erected as idols or of those values that a culture assumes as absolute even though they are not. The Church has the mission of bearing witness to the "true God and the only Lord." (*Puebla Document*, No. 405)

---

[13] "La Iglesia parte en su evangelización de aquellas semillas esparcidas por Cristo."

Framing the task in more positive terms, when evangelizing, "the Church seeks the renewal, elevation and perfection of cultures through the active presence of the Risen One, center of history, and of his Spirit" (*Puebla Document*, No. 407).

"Seeds of the Word" appears only once more in the Puebla Document, this time as *semillas del Verbo*, rather than as *gérmenes del Verbo* (the expression used in *Puebla Document*, No. 401), and this time in the context of a discussion of popular religion. The bishops affirm that popular religion is not only an object of evangelization, and also that, inasmuch as it incarnates the Word of God (*contiene encarnada la Palabra de Dios*), it is an active means by which people are continually evangelizing themselves (*con la cual el pueblo se evangeliza continuamente a sí mismo*) (*Puebla Document*, No. 450). They then observe that these practices of Catholic popular religion (*piedad popular católica*) have not (yet) reached "some cultural groups of autochthonous or of African origin, who for their part have rich values and hold on to seeds of the Word as they await the living Word" (*Puebla Document*, No. 451). While "seeds of the Word" are not mere culturally specific placeholders or temporary stand-ins before the reception of the "living Word" that is the focus and the goal of evangelization, the bishops affirm that these "seeds" are oriented toward and compatible with the work of evangelization and its outcomes.

Medellín 1968

The final document that emerged from CELAM's Second General Conference in Medellín in 1968 mentions "seeds of the Word" only once, in Part Six, which is devoted to "*Pastoral Popular*."[14] This section, which begins by setting the scene for

---

[14] Second General Conference of Latin American Bishops, Final Document, Medellín, Colombia, September 1968, http://www.celam.org/ doc_conferencias/Documento_Conclusivo_Medellin.pdf. Translations

pastoral activity, acknowledges the considerable variety of the conditions of faith, the beliefs, and the Christian practices among the people of Latin America. These range, in the words of the bishops, from "semipagan ethnic groups" (*grupos étnicos semipaganizados*), to "groups of *campesinos* who maintain a profound sense of religiosity, to marginalized groups whose practice of Christianity is at a very low level even though they have religious sensibilities" (*Medellín Document,* Sec. VI, No. 1). This utterly disparaging characterization is followed in the same paragraph by the simple statement that "There is a process of cultural and religious transformation," and then a call for rethinking pastoral activity that adapts to the diversity and cultural pluralism of the people of Latin America.

The bishops cautioned, "When judging popular religiosity, we cannot start from a westernized cultural interpretation, typical of the urban middle and upper classes, but rather from the meaning that this religiosity has in the context of the subculture of marginalized rural and urban groups" (*Medellín Document*, Sec. VI, No. 1). What follows, sadly though perhaps not surprisingly, reflects the elitist negative attitude with which the bishops regarded the religious practices of ordinary people:

> Their expressions may be distorted and mixed to a certain extent with an ancestral religious heritage, where tradition exercises an almost tyrannical power; they have the danger of being easily influenced by magical practices and superstitions that reveal a rather utilitarian character and a certain fear of the divine, which require the intercession of beings closer to humans and more malleable [*plásticas*] and concrete expressions. These religious expressions can, however, be babblings [*balbuceos*] of an authentic

mine. Subsequent references to this document will appear parenthetically in the text as *Medellín Document*.

religiosity, expressed with the cultural elements that are available. (*Medellín Document*, Sec. VI, No. 4)

This is entirely lacking in the "deep attitude of love" on which the Latin American bishops eventually came to insist (at Puebla) as the optics through which the work of evangelization should view culture. About practices of popular religion that they characterize as "distorted and mixed to a certain extent with an ancestral religious heritage, where tradition exercises an almost tyrannical power," the most that the bishops are willing to concede in the Medellín Document is that these "religious expressions" can be (though not necessarily), infantile babblings of "authentic religiosity" that make do with "the cultural elements that are available." Following this unflattering characterization of popular religion comes the observation that faith always reaches people "wrapped in a cultural language, and so in natural religiosity it is possible to find the seeds [*gérmenes*] of a call from God" (*Medellín Document*, Sec. VI, No. 4).[15] The bishops concede,

---

[15] The consideration of "Pastoral Popular" in Part Six of the Medellín Document is followed by a treatment of "Pastoral de las Elites" in Part Seven. On the treatment of popular religion at Medellín, Puebla, and Santo Domingo, see Orlando O. Espín, *Grace and Humanness: Theological Reflections Because of Culture* (Maryknoll, NY: Orbis Books, 2007), chap. 5, "From Medellín to Santo Domingo," 120–145. Also see Orlando O. Espín, *The Faith of the People: Theological Reflections on Popular Catholicism* (Maryknoll, NY: Orbis Books, 1997). Also see Rebecca M. Berrú-Davis, "Theologizing Popular Catholicism," in *The Wiley Blackwell Companion to Latino/a Theology*, ed. Orlando O. Espín (Oxford, UK: Wiley-Blackwell, 2015), 387–400. The close and careful attention to popular religion in the work of Espín and other U.S. Latin@ theologians is, in the words of Carmen Nanko-Fernández, "a departure from the disdain or indifference expressed toward popular religion by the strands of Latin American liberation theology most known to English speakers" (Nanko-Fernández, "Lo Cotidiano as Locus Theologicus," in *The Wiley Blackwell Companion to Latino/a Theology*, 27). That disdain is plainly evident in the *Puebla Document*.

using the language of sowing seeds, that "Faith, and consequently the Church, are sown and grow in the culturally diverse religiosity of the peoples. This faith, though imperfect, can still be found in the lower cultural levels."

The Medellín Document then outlines how evangelization should engage with popular religion, using language that is drawn directly from the documents of the Second Vatican Council, with four brief quotations in the course of a single paragraph. This engagement should

> discover in that religiosity the secret presence of God, the ray of truth which enlightens all [*people*] with the light of the Word, present already before the incarnation and the apostolic preaching, and make that seed bear fruit. Without breaking the broken reed and without extinguishing the smoldering wick, the Church accepts with joy and respect, purifies and incorporates into the order of faith, the various religious and human elements that are hidden in that religiosity as seeds of the Word and that constitute or may constitute a preparation for the Gospel. (*Medellín Document*, Sec. VI, No. 5)

"Secret presence of God" comes from the Decree on the Missionary Activity of the Church (*Ad Gentes*): "By the preaching of the word and by the celebration of the sacraments... He [*God*] brings about the presence of Christ, the author of salvation. But whatever truth and grace are to be found among the nations, as a sort of *secret presence of God*, He frees from all taint of evil and restores to Christ its maker."[16] "Ray of truth which enlightens

---

[16] Second Vatican Council, Decree on the Missionary Activity of the Church (*Ad Gentes*), December 7, 1965. No. 9, https://www.vatican.va/archive/hist_councils/ii_vatican_council/documents/vat-ii_decree_19651207_ad-gentes_en.html

all" comes from the Council's Declaration of the Relation of the
Church to Non-Christian Religions (*Nostra Aetate*):

> other religions found everywhere try to counter the rest-
> lessness of the human heart, each in its own manner, by
> proposing "ways," comprising teachings, rules of life, and
> sacred rites. The Catholic Church rejects nothing that is
> true and holy in these religions. She regards with sincere
> reverence those ways of conduct and of life, those precepts
> and teachings which, though differing in many aspects
> from the ones she holds and sets forth, nonetheless often
> reflect a *ray of that truth* which enlightens all.[17]

"Seeds of the Word" comes from *Ad Gentes*, where the expression appears in the context of the decree's Article 1, on Christian
witness:

> In order that they [*the children of the Church*] may be able
> to bear more fruitful witness to Christ, let them be joined
> to those men by esteem and love; let them acknowledge
> themselves to be members of the group of men among
> whom they live; let them share in cultural and social life by
> the various undertakings and enterprises of human living;
> let them be familiar with their national and religious tradi-
> tions; let them gladly and reverently lay bare *the seeds of the*
> *Word* which lie hidden among their fellows. (No. 11)

Finally, the mention of "preparation for the Gospel" (*praepa-*
ratio evangelica) comes from *Ad Gentes:*

---

[17] Second Vatican Council, Declaration of the Relation of the Church
to Non-Christian Religions (*Nostra Aetate*), October 28, 1965, No. 2,
https://www.vatican.va/archive/hist_councils/ii_vatican_council/docu-
ments/vat-ii_decl_19651028_nostra-aetate_en.html

This universal design of God for the salvation of the human race is carried out not only, as it were, secretly in the soul of a man, or by the attempts (even religious ones by which in diverse ways it seeks after God) if perchance it may contact Him or find Him, though He be not far from anyone of us (cf. Acts 17:27). For these attempts need to be enlightened and healed; even though, through the kindly workings of Divine Providence, they may sometimes serve as leading strings toward God, or as a *preparation for the Gospel.* (No. 3)

This catena of quotations from the documents of the Second Vatican Council, however brief each may be, leaves not the slightest doubt that the intention of the bishops at Medellín was to implement the Council in their Latin American context. In the course of only two sentences, they weave together the Council's emphases on the Church's relationship with non-Christian religions and on evangelization vis-à-vis indigenous religious practices and popular religion. In spite of the negative attitude that the Medellín Document exhibits toward practices that reflect Latin America's indigenous religious heritage, the bishops quote Matthew 12:20 (which is a citation of Isaiah 42:3), to indicate the sensitivity that is called for in accepting, purifying, and incorporating the "seeds of the Word" that are manifest in Latin American popular religion. They also recognize the need to seek out "the ray of truth which enlightens all" which was present in Latin America even "before the incarnation and before the apostolic preaching." The bishops affirm unequivocally that this "ray of truth" was shining the light of the Word on the indigenous peoples of Latin America well before the arrival of the European colonizers and missionaries.

From the Final Document of the Amazonian Synod, back to Aparecida in 2007, to Santo Domingo in 1992, Puebla in 1979,

and Medellín in 1968, "seeds of the Word" is the expression that
the bishops of Latin America consistently chose to describe the
activity of God among the indigenous peoples of Latin America
prior to 1492 and in the practices of popular religion both past
and present. They cautiously avoid naming the divine activity
of sowing the seeds of the Word as revelation, insisting that the
seeds of the Word in indigenous cultures and present in indigenous traditions, values, and religious practices predisposed the
peoples of Latin America to receive the proclamation of the
Gospel. Yet it is hard to avoid the impression that the expression
implies an indigenous incarnation of sorts whereby the Word
finds efficacious expression in the indigenous vernaculars of Latin
America, something over and above the activity of the Word in
creation (as in John 1:3). While the use of the expression by the
Latin American bishops from Medellín through Aparecida is
distinctive with regard to the value it places on indigenous Latin
American cultures, values, and practices, and while that carries
over to the use of "seeds of the Word" at the Amazonian Synod,
in all of these documents the bishops took their cues from the
way this expression was used in *Ad Gentes*. How "seeds of the
Word" made it into *Ad Gentes* and where the expression came
from in the first place are worth exploring.

Seeds of the Word:
The Second Vatican Council

The phrase "seeds of the Word," appears only twice in the documents of the Second Vatican Council, and both occurrences are in *Ad
Gentes*, in No. 11, reproduced above, and in No. 15, reproduced below.

When the Holy Spirit, who calls all men in Christ and
arouses in their hearts the submission of faith by the *seed
of the word* and the preaching of the Gospel, brings those

who believe in Christ to a new life through the womb of
the baptismal font, he gathers them into one people of God
which is "a chosen race, a royal priesthood, a holy nation, a
purchased people" (1 Pet 2:9). (No. 15)[18]

As José Luis Moreno explains, this wording did not make its
appearance until the sixth redaction of the schema for *Ad Gentes*
that was sent to the Council Fathers on May 28, 1965. It was
added as the result of a new sensitivity among the Council Fathers
to the relationship between the Gospel and culture.[19] Moreno
identifies the interventions of three non-European bishops as the
catalysts that moved the document in this direction. The first was
an observation by the Archbishop of Delhi, Angel Fernandes, who
wrote that "The Church as Catholic is nowhere a stranger, but
recognizes and favors the true values of all cultures, assumes them,
imbues them with Christian principles and elevates them . . . and
thus the whole Church is enriched with the goods of the various
cultures."[20] The second was an oral intervention by Cardinal
Laurean Rugambwa, a native of present-day Tanzania and Africa's
first cardinal, in which he explained how the work of missionaries
flourished among peoples whose values they recognized with reverence. Calling for cultural adaptation, he noted that

---

[18] The translation of *Ad Gentes* No. 15 is from Austin Flannery, ed.,
Vatican Council II: The Conciliar and Post-Conciliar Documents (Colleg-
eville, MN: Liturgical Press, 1980). The English translation of *Ad Gentes*
No. 15 found on the Vatican website at http://www.vatican.va/archive/
hist_councils/ii_vatican_council/documents/vat-ii_decree_19651207_
ad-gentes_en.html is seriously defective, as accessed on March 20, 2021.

[19] José Luis Moreno, "'Semina Verbi' de San Justino al Vaticano II,"
in *Dios en la Palabra y en la Historia. Actas del XIII Simposio Internacional
de Teología de la Universidad de Navarra*, ed. César Izquierdo (Pamplona,
Spain: Editorial Universidad de Navarra, 1993), 127.

[20] As quoted in Moreno, "'Semina Verbi,'" 128. All translations from
Moreno are mine.

Adaptation requires, above all, that the moral and religious values that constitute the inner core of each culture be recognized and accepted. In the moral and religious treasure of each people there are many good, healthy and beautiful things that developed through the centuries according to the mysterious plan of God, so that at the divinely established time they would be included in the Body of Christ, which is the Church, and so in it receive admirable elevation.[21]

It was in his intervention that Egyptian-born Melkite bishop Elias Zoghby introduced the expression "seeds of the Word" into the discussion, with insights enriched by references to the patristic tradition:

The redemptive mission of Christ and the Church refers to humanity that has already been fertilized by the divine seed, by the germs of the Word (in Greek *spermata tou Logou*), as Justin, Clement of Alexandria, and Origen say. The evangelizer who arrives in a land that has not yet been evangelized sows the seed of the Word in souls that are not completely alien to the Word of God, but rather have been prepared for a long time by the Holy Spirit, since those souls received from their creation the creative Word, that is, the divine seed, waiting for the dew of a new dawn to grow and bear fruit.[22]

Insisting that there is no split between the creative Word and the redeeming Word, Zoghby went on to explain:

Just as the Word, by giving life, planted the "seed of the Word" in every human being, so also by the incarnation of

---

[21] As quoted in Moreno, "'Semina Verbi,'" 128.
[22] As quoted in Moreno, "'Semina Verbi,'" 129.

the Word and by redemption, every human being received the fullness of life. That is to say, the light that existed in the beginning shone in the incarnation; the seed of the Word is given in the incarnation, but the fullness of the Word is granted to us in redemption: "From his fullness we have all received grace upon grace."[23]

Zoghby aptly concludes his insistence on the connections between the order of creation and the order of redemption with a quotation from the prologue of the Fourth Gospel (John 1:16). Focusing on the relevance this has for the Church's missionary activity, he goes on to insist that the missionary Church should assign

great importance to the seed of the Word hidden in every person and to the progressive action of God in the human race, that is, to the pedagogy of God. The Church evangelizing among the peoples in the villages to evangelize must first discover that divine seed and the natural riches which that seed has produced.[24]

The missionary Church, Zoghby went on to insist, should not impose a "prefabricated Christ," and the peoples who receive Jesus Christ by faith must express and reincarnate him in their image and likeness so that he might truly be all in all," citing 1 Corinthians 15:28. Finally, in a remarkable statement that anticipates by more than half a century the polyhedric model of intercultural *encuentro* proposed by Pope Francis, Zoghby insisted that

It is not enough for the evangelized peoples to receive the Church's proclamation of the Gospel, for they too can and must enrich the Church. And they will enrich the Church

---

[23] As quoted in Moreno, "'Semina Verbi,'" 129.
[24] As quoted in Moreno, "'Semina Verbi,'" 130.

not only by the faith they receive from it, but also by contributing their own values received from God with the seed of the Word and cultivated through the centuries by the divine pedagogy of the Spirit.[25]

Zoghby's intervention, together with those of Fernandes and Rugambwa, significantly influenced the formulation of *Ad Gentes* No. 11 and No. 15. It is worth noting, though, that their contributions to the shaping of *Ad Gentes*, including Zoghby's suggestive invocation of "seeds of the Word" were focused on the Church's missionary activity and not on interreligious dialogue. The same is true, by and large, of how the expression is used in the final documents of the four CELAM General Conferences we have examined. This is confirmed at least indirectly by the way that the bishops carefully avoid mentioning "revelation" in the same breath as "seeds of the word," preferring instead to frame that expression in terms of evangelization both past and present and its engagement with indigenous and African descendant Latin Americans. Only the Medellín Final Document combines a phrase from *Nostra Aetate* 2 ("ray of truth which enlightens all") with a reference to "seeds of the Word" from *Ad Gentes*.

Even so, Moreno points to a few noteworthy but little-known instances where Justin Martyr was invoked with a broader horizon in mind than evangelization or missionary activity *per se*, not in the documents of the Council themselves but in the lively discussions that were taking place around and about what the Council's concerns and priorities should be. Among these was a suggestion that came from the Catholic University of Leopoldville (Congo): "We hope that the Council ... will declare that even in non-Christian religions it is possible to recognize the influence of supernatural grace and, even more,

---

[25] As quoted in Moreno, "'Semina Verbi,'" 130.

a preparation for the Gospel."[26] The suggestion is accompanied by a reference to Justin's Second Apology, No. 13. Moreno mentions another intervention of Cardinal Rugambwa, this time commenting on what the focus ought to be for the Council's decree on ecumenism: "In the missionary field there is already a traditional norm, which has been known since the beginnings of the Church: see, for example, the works of Saint Justin and other Fathers of the Church; and this rule is: 'what there is of truth and goodness on earth and in the human heart is of Christ, it is the seed of the Word.'"[27]

Moreno also reports the comments of the Archbishop of Santiago, Chile, Raúl Silva Henríquez, about the direction that the Council's decree on religious freedom should adopt:

> The human understanding has an innate appetite for truth. This is the case not only for the truths of the natural order, but also for the truth of the Catholic religion, because all people have been created structurally oriented to obtain the vision of the Father in Christ and by his grace. This is the Church's ancient doctrine of the Church that was expressed in the theology of San Justin about the *Logos spermatikos* and in the saying of Tertullian about the naturally Christian soul.[28]

In an impressive feat of bibliographical archaeology, Moreno proposes that it was Henri de Lubac's 1938 book, *Catholicisme: Les aspects sociaux du dogme* that prompted ideas like these, noting that de Lubac's book was probably the first—and perhaps even the only—theological work prior to the Second Vatican Council that applied Justin's concept of "seeds of the Word" to

---

[26] As quoted in Moreno, "'Semina Verbi,'" 133.
[27] As quoted in Moreno, "'Semina Verbi,'" 134.
[28] As quoted in Moreno, "'Semina Verbi,'" 134.

non-Christian religions and to call for a positive evaluation of these religions.[29]

Moreno points out that while the expression "seeds of the Word" appears in the documents of Vatican II in those exact words only in *Ad Gentes*, the sense of it is echoed in a number of other places that draw on language taken from the same semantic field.[30] This includes *Ad Gentes* No.18, in which members of religious institutes are invited to "reflect attentively on how Christian religious life might be able to assimilate the ascetic and contemplative traditions, whose seeds were sometimes planted by God in ancient cultures already prior to the preaching of the Gospel." *Ad Gentes* No. 19 then discusses how the Church is planted and takes root in specific communities with their own local cultures. *Ad Gentes* No. 22 then speaks of how the "seed which is the word of God, watered by divine dew, sprouts from the good ground and draws from thence its moisture, which it transforms and assimilates into itself, and finally bears much fruit." Elaborating on that metaphor, the decree continues by saying that, "In harmony with

---

[29] Moreno, "'Semina Verbi,'" 134. See Henri de Lubac, *Catholicism: Christ and the Common Destiny of Man*, trans. Lancelot C. Sheppard and Sister Elizabeth Englund (San Francisco, CA: Ignatius Press, 1988), especially 282–302. De Lubac writes, "Ever since the day when, full of strength and the promises of the Holy Spirit, the Church issued from the Cenacle to overrun the earth, she has encountered everywhere in her progress countries that are already, in the religious sense, occupied. Now the religions with which she comes in conflict are by no means, for their respective peoples, just like a cloak that they have merely to put off. Customs, traditions, social and intellectual life, morality, all bear their imprint. . . . Must everything be jettisoned to give way to the Gospel?" He answers no, going on to explain that "Human reason is weak and wavering, but it is not entirely doomed to error, and it is not possible for the divinity to be entirely hidden from it. '*The seed of the Word is innate in the whole human race.*' The divine likeness in it may be dimmed, veiled, disfigured, but it is always there" (282–283). Here de Lubac notes a reference to Justin's Second Apology 8, 1.

[30] Moreno, "'Semina Verbi,'" 132.

the economy of the Incarnation, the young churches . . . borrow from the customs and traditions of their people, from their wisdom and their learning, from their arts and disciplines, all those things which can contribute to the glory of their Creator, or enhance the grace of their Savior, or dispose Christian life the way it should be" (*Ad Gentes*, No. 22). The language of seed and soil is used to articulate a vision for the growth of local churches that is rooted in their particular customs and traditions, or—in other words—their local vernaculars. The image of sowing seed appears with similar intent in the Dogmatic Constitution on the Church (*Lumen Gentium*) which says of the Church's work in evangelization "that whatever good is found sown in the minds and hearts of [*people*] or in the rites and customs of peoples, these are not only preserved from destruction, but are purified, raised up, and perfected for the glory of God, the confusion of the devil, and the happiness of [*humankind*]."[31]

In *Gaudium et Spes* under the heading of "Some Principles for the Proper Development of Culture," the Council expresses a Eurocentric notion of "high culture" by suggesting that when people devote themselves to such disciplines as philosophy, history, mathematics, and the natural sciences, and to the cultivation of the arts, this helps to "elevate the human family to a more sublime understanding of truth, goodness, and beauty, and to the formation of considered opinions which have universal value" (No. 57).

---

[31] This translation of *Lumen Gentium* No. 17 is from Flannery, ed., *Vatican Council II*. The English translation at the Vatican website http://www.vatican.va/archive/hist_councils/ii_vatican_council/documents/vat-ii_const_19641121_lumen-gentium_en.html does not completely reflect the wording of the Latin original: "Opera autem sua efficit ut quidquid boni in corde menemque huminum vel in propriis ritibus et culturis populorum *seminatum* invenitur, non tantum ut pereat, sed sanetur, elevetur et consummetur ad gloriam Dei, confusionem daemonis et beatitudinem hominis."

Through such activity, human beings "may be more clearly enlightened by that marvelous Wisdom which was with God from all eternity." Here, quoting Proverbs 8:1, the Council underscores the activity of divine wisdom in the work of creation before citing John 1:9–10. By engaging in the disciplines of the mind and of the arts, human beings can be "more easily drawn to the worship and contemplation of the Creator," and, by grace, disposed to acknowledge the Word of God, who before he became flesh in order to save all and to sum up all in Himself was already 'in the world' as 'the true light which enlightens every[one]."[32] Here the references to Proverbs 8:31 and John 1:9–10 complement each other to emphasize the activity of divine wisdom/word before the Incarnation.

"Seeds of the Word" is notably and somewhat curiously absent from the Council's Dogmatic Constitution on Divine Revelation. While that absence is not insignificant, it should not lead us to dismiss the value of this expression for understanding divine self-disclosure. As already noted, *Dei Verbum*'s treatment of revelation itself in chapter one cites John 1:3 and Romans 1:19–20 to underline the activity of the Word in the work of creation before the incarnation and the witness that creation itself offers to the Creator. Curiously, though, there is no mention of "seeds of the Word" as the divinely inspired disposition by which it has always been possible for people everywhere to make the connection between creation and the Creator. It is just as curious that, as Néstor Medina points out, *Dei Verbum* "does not deal with the connection between cultures and divine revelation."[33] When *Dei Verbum* does mention culture, it is in the context of the efforts

---

[32] On the theme of culture in *Gaudium et Spes*, see Néstor Medina, *Christianity, Empire, and the Spirit: (Re)Configuring Faith and the Cultural* (Leiden: Brill, 2018), 275–280. Also see Robert J. Schreiter, "Faith and Cultures: Challenges to a World Church," *Theological Studies* 50 (1989), esp. 750.

[33] Medina, *Christianity, Empire, and the Spirit*, 273.

by interpreters of the Bible "to search out the intention of the sacred writers." In so doing, "The interpreter must investigate what meaning the sacred writer[s] intended to express and actually expressed in particular circumstances by using contemporary literary forms in accordance with the situation of [*their*] own time and culture" (*Dei Verbum*, No. 12).

Medina is right: *Dei Verbum* does not deal with the relationship between divine revelation and cultures with specific attention to the addressees of divine revelation. Yet it is important to recognize that the document is a product of its times, times in which the historical critical approach to biblical interpretation was struggling to make headway among Catholic exegetes, and so the promulgation of *Dei Verbum* represented a formal endorsement after more than half a century of resistance from Rome.[34] It would take time for the approach to culture that began to develop in *Gaudium et Spes* to make it into Roman Catholic approaches to biblical studies. That is because it would only be later that biblical interpretation would pivot from almost exclusive attention to author-centered approaches to the text toward reading strategies that are reader-centered, beginning first with literary critical models that emphasized synchronic approaches to the biblical text and eventually came to focus on "flesh and blood" readers with attention to their social location, including all that is included under the broad rubric of culture.[35] Given the

---

[34] See Joseph A. Fitzmyer, *The Biblical Commission's Document "The Interpretation of the Bible in the Church"* (Rome: Biblical Institute Press, 1995); idem, *The Interpretation of Scripture: In Defense of the Historical-Critical Method* (Mahwah, NJ: Paulist Press, 2008).

[35] See Fernando F. Segovia and Mary Ann Tolbert, eds., *Reading from this Place, Volume 1: Social Location and Biblical Interpretation in the United States* (Minneapolis: Augsburg Fortress, 1995); idem, *Reading from this Place, Volume 2: Social Location and Biblical Interpretation in Global Perspective* (Minneapolis, MN: Augsburg Fortress, 2000). Also see Jean-Pierre Ruiz, "The Bible and Latino/a Theology," in *The Wiley Blackwell Companion to Latino/a Theology*, 111–127; Francisco Lozada Jr.,

profile of Roman Catholic biblical studies at the time of the Second
Vatican Council, it would have been surprising to see *Dei Verbum*
pay attention to "seeds of the Word" as *Ad Gentes* did, with its focus
on the Church's missionary activity and on the dynamics of evangelization in the worlds in front of the biblical text.

With all this in mind, it makes sense to turn from the use of
"seeds of the Word" in CELAM and in the documents of Vatican
II to attend to the origins of the expression in the work of Justin
Martyr and to consider what has been made of that metaphor.

Justin Martyr and the Seeds of the Word

In his Second Apology (8, 1), Justin Martyr wrote, "In every
person a seed of the Word is implanted."[36] Later on in the Second
Apology (13), he elaborates:

> I confess and I both pray and with all my strength strive
> to be found a Christian; not because the teachings of
> Plato are different from those of Christ, but because they
> are not in every respect equal, as neither are those of the
> others, Stoics, and poets, and historians. For each person
> spoke well, according to the part present in [*them*] of the
> divine logos, the Sower . . . whatever things were rightly
> said among all people are the property of us Christians.
> For next to God, we worship and love the logos who is

"Reinventing the Biblical Tradition: An Exploration of Social Location
Hermeneutics," in *Futuring Our Past: Explorations in the Theology of Tradition,* ed. Orlando O. Espín and Gary Macy (Maryknoll, NY: Orbis Books,
2006), 113–140; Jacqueline M. Hidalgo, *Latina/o/x Studies and Biblical
Studies* (Leiden: Brill, 2020).

[36] As quoted in Ragnar Holte, "Logos Spermatikos: Christianity and
Ancient Philosophy according to St. Justin's Apologies," *Studia Theologica*
12, no. 1 (1958): 133.

from the unbegotten and ineffable God, since He also became [*incarnate*] for our sakes, that, becoming a partaker of our sufferings, he might also bring us healing. For all the writers were able to see realities darkly, through the presence in them of an implanted seed of logos. For the seed and imitation of something, imparted according to capacity, is one thing, and another is the thing itself, the part possession and imitation of which is effected according to the grace coming from him.[37]

What relevance could these words from the writings of a second-century apologist, with his talk of Plato and the Stoics, possibly have for twentieth- and twenty-first-century Latin America? How might Justin's words about seeds of the Word help us map an understanding of revelation that draws on a sixteenth-century *encuentro* on Mona Island between indigenous Taínos and Spanish colonizers, along with the beginnings of a hermeneutics of the vernacular in sixteenth-century Spain, as well as a 2019 gathering in Rome that focused on Amazonia? This is the itinerary across time and space that is proposed in these pages. After all, "For Christians of the patristic era, to consider the possible salvation of non-Christians never meant seeking any salvific good in pagan religious practice."[38] Had "seeds of the Word" not been invoked in the Concluding Document of the Amazonian Synod, Justin would likely be no more than a brief footnote in this book, if he were to be mentioned at all.

As Ragnar Holte explains, albeit in somewhat archaic language, "By the middle of the second century A.D., Christianity

---

[37] St. Justin Martyr, *The First and Second Apologies*, trans. Leslie William Barnard, Ancient Christian Writers, 56 (New York: Paulist Press, 1997), 83–84.

[38] Joseph Carola, "Non-Christians in Patristic Theology," in *Catholic Engagement with World Religions*, ed. Karl J. Becker and Ilaria Morali (Maryknoll, NY: Orbis Books, 2010), 34.

had expanded to such an extent over the ancient world that a theological confrontation with the contemporary heathen culture and
learning was absolutely necessary."[39] The notion of the *logos sper-*
matikos advanced by Justin Martyr (ca. 100–ca. 165 CE) was one
important contribution to the early engagement of Christianity
with Hellenistic philosophy.[40] Holte summarizes Justin's position in the First and Second Apology in these terms: according to
Justin, while Christians are in possession of the whole truth, there
are certain similar teachings to be found outside of Christianity.
This is because the *Logos* which was fully revealed only with the
Incarnation, "has nevertheless been partly perceptible through the
seed of *Logos* (*to sperma tou logou*) implanted in all men from the
time of the Creation."[41] Justin also maintained that the Old Testament was the source from which Greek philosophers drew their
teachings, and that demons are to blame for such distortions of
Christian teaching as are found among them.[42]

Holte goes on to clarify how, for Justin, "The glimpses of truth,
perceived by the philosophers through their participation in Logos
Spermatikos, are Christian property, because the Christians are the
only people who love and worship the incarnate *Logos*."[43] Holte
cautions against imagining that Justin was trying "to find a way to

---

[39] Holte, "Logos Spermatikos," 109.

[40] For a concise overview of Justin's contribution, see Carola, "Non-
Christians in Patristic Theology," in *Catholic Engagement with World Religions*,
34–37. For more on Justin, also see L. W. Bernard, *Justin Martyr: His Life
and Thought* (Cambridge, UK: Cambridge University Press, 1967), especially
85–100; Mark J. Edwards, "Justin's Logos and the Word of God," *Journal of
Early Christian Studies*, 3, no. 3 (Fall 1995): 261–280; Wendy Elgersma
Helleman, "Justin Martyr and the 'Logos': An Apologetical Strategy," *Philoso-
phia Reformata* 67, no. 2 (2002): 128–147; Eric Osborn, "Justin Martyr and
the Logos Spermatikos," *Studia Missionalia* 42 (1993): 143–159.

[41] Holte, "Logos Spermatikos," 111.

[42] Holte, "Logos Spermatikos," 111.

[43] Holte, "Logos Spermatikos," 112.

reconcile Christianity to Ancient philosophy, or even to assign to the latter an independent character of revelation."[44] Scholars who favor this view, Holte concludes, are merely trying to (mis)construe Justin "as an exponent of their own theological viewpoint."[45] According to Holte, the revelation available through the activity of the *Logos spermatikos* is limited to the sort of natural revelation that is mentioned in Romans 1:18–20 and Acts 17.[46]

Joseph Carola tells us that, according to Justin, "The seminal *logos* is the principle of natural revelation. It accounts for the innate religious and moral sense that human beings possess. Constituted by the seminal *logos*, human reason can attain to a knowledge of God's existence and the universal moral law."[47] Carola also points out the important distinction in Justin's writings between the *logos spermatikos* and the *sperma tou logou,* the latter of which is present in every human being. As Carola explains, *logos spermatikos* "refers specifically to the Divine Word . . . the *logos spermatikos* is not disseminated but rather actively disseminates or sows his seed (*sperma tou logou* [*seeds of the word*]), which is other than himself. Thus does he illuminate human beings morally and religiously."[48] Citing Holte with approval, Carola points out an important distinction. According to Justin, "The *sperma tou logou,*" the seed of the Word, "is neither the *logos* himself nor a part of him sown in human beings, but rather an imitation of the *logos*—'a knowledge,' Holte argues, 'in which he is reflected.'"[49]

Given the popularity acquired by the expression he coined, even though it occurred as such only twice in the documents of

---

[44] Holte, "Logos Spermatikos," 112.

[45] Holte, "Logos Spermatikos," 113.

[46] Holte, "Logos Spermatikos," 128–130.

[47] Carola, "Non-Christians in Patristic Theology," 35.

[48] Carola, "Non-Christians in Patristic Theology," 36.

[49] Carola, "Non-Christians in Patristic Theology," 36, referring to Holte, "Logos Spermatikos," 146.

Vatican II, Justin has sometimes been enlisted as something of a forerunner of interreligious inclusivism. For example, Paul Knitter writes about how, during the early centuries of Christianity,

> They coined a new expression (or better, symbol) the
> *logos spermatikos*. . . . All Christians experienced that the
> Word of God was "made flesh" in Jesus. Now they were
> saying that before Jesus, and still throughout the Greco-
> Roman world, this same Word of God was scattered
> like seeds. Concentrated in Jesus, it was also thrown to
> the winds of history. This universally sown Word is "the
> Word of which all humankind partakes." One of the
> Fathers, Justin Martyr, could even say that anyone who
> hears God's call in this Seed-Word and tries to follow its
> lead is really already a Christian, even though she never
> heard of Jesus.[50]

Knitter goes on to propose that while these early Christians "went on to insist that the Seed-Word in other cultures and religions needs to be clarified and fulfilled in the fully embodied Word in Jesus, this was still a strong affirmation of God's saving presence beyond the church."[51] An attentive reading of Justin leads to a reserved "yes, but" assessment of Knitter's claim about the inclusive breadth of Justin's thinking. There is in fact a broad range of views about how inclusive Justin may have been. On the one hand, Henry Chadwick claimed that "Of all the early Christian theologians Justin is the most optimistic about the harmony of Christianity

---

[50]   Paul F. Knitter, *Introducing Theologies of Religion* (Maryknoll, NY: Orbis Books, 2014), 65. Also see Cullan Joyce, "The Seeds of Dialogue in Justin Martyr," *Australian eJournal of Theology* 7 (June 2006), https://www.researchgate.net/publication/265200741_The_Seeds_of_Dialogue_in_Justin_Martyr

[51]   Knitter, *Introducing Theologies of Religion*, 65.

and Greek philosophy."[52] He further maintained that for Justin, "Plato and Christ can be reconciled, with few qualifications," and "the gospel and the best of pagan philosophers give almost identical ways of apprehending the same truth."[53] Holte represents the very opposite position, firmly insisting instead that "Justin's Logos Spermatikos theory is not intended to grant a character of revelation to religious or philosophical systems in their entirety. It is strictly limited to a few conceptions, i.e., certain ideas on God and on the falsity of idolatry and also certain basic moral conceptions." Holte is willing to concede nothing more than "Justin can scarcely be said to have essentially extended the content of St. Paul's thoughts on a natural revelation."[54] Wendy Elgersma Helleman comes to a more nuanced conclusion than either Chadwick or Holte. Contra Holte, she maintains that "Justin clearly does not want to close the door on pagans having some accurate knowledge about God," while, contra Chadwick, she affirms that "Justin is clear in putting Christian knowledge of God on a very different plane. Christians not only have full access to truth; they are healed of diseases and released from demonically inspired deception."[55]

---

[52] Henry Chadwick, *Early Christian Thought and the Classical Tradition* (Oxford: Clarendon Press, 1966), 7.

[53] As quoted in Helleman, "Justin Martyr and the 'Logos,'" 132.

[54] Holte, "'Logos Spermatikos,'" 163.

[55] Helleman, "Justin Martyr and the 'Logos,'" 145. Helleman summarizes Justin's overall apologetic purpose: "In an environment in which Christians were regarded as [*mad*], Justin made every effort to show that they had good reason for their views and practice.... If Christian accounts can be shown to be analogue to teachings of Greek poets and philosophers, why are Christians so unjustly hated and pursued, when the former are not?" (146–147). Also see Pierre Ndoumaï, "Justin Martyr et le dialogue interreligieux contemporain," *Laval théologique et philosophique* 66, no. 3 (2010): 547–564. Justin Keith goes a bit too far in flatly asserting that Justin "was no exception to the exclusivism of mainline Christians of this period" ("Justin Martyr and Religious Exclusivism," in *One God, One Lord: Christianity in a World of Religious Pluralism*, ed. Andrew D. Clarke and

Growing the Seeds: Amplifying Justin

While it would be anachronistic to characterize Justin as something of a proto-inclusivist, there is no doubt that "seeds of the Word" as invoked by Vatican II in *Ad Gentes* significantly amplifies the theological significance of the expression he coined to include, as Moreno has suggested:

1. "everything good and true that is in the mind, the heart, and the soul of every person;"
2. "the specific values of cultures: their cultural, moral, religious, and spiritual patrimony; customs, traditions, wisdom, teachings, arts, and institutions that are specific to each people;"
3. "the values of each religion: religious efforts to seek God, ascetic and contemplative religious traditions, rituals and moral and religious values."[56]

The Church's task vis-à-vis these "seeds of the Word," is to recognize and preserve them, to study and promote them with sincerity, joy, respect, and reverence; to take them up and integrate them into Christian faith proper and its expressions; and to bring them to their fullness and development, which is the Gospel and the Christian life.[57] Moreno accurately concludes that while Vatican II broadened the sense of "seeds of the Word" beyond Justin, the Council's amplification is not in tension with the basic direction of Justin's development of this concept.[58]

Subsequent affirmation of the Council's amplification of Justin's concept can be found, for example, in *Evangelii Nuntiandi* 53, where Paul VI wrote:

Bruce W. Winter [Grand Rapids, MI: Baker, 1992], 185).

[56] Moreno, "'Semina Verbi,'" 135.

[57] Moreno, "'Semina Verbi,'" 135.

[58] Moreno, "'Semina Verbi,'" 138.

This first proclamation [*of Jesus Christ*] is also addressed to the immense sections of mankind who practice non-Christian religions. The Church respects and esteems these non-Christian religions because they are the living expression of the soul of vast groups of people. They carry within them the echo of thousands of years of searching for God, a quest which is incomplete but often made with great sincerity and righteousness of heart. They possess an impressive patrimony of deeply religious texts. They have taught generations of people how to pray. They are all impregnated with innumerable "seeds of the Word" and can constitute a true "preparation for the Gospel," to quote a felicitous term used by the Second Vatican Council and borrowed from Eusebius of Caesarea.[59]

As we have already seen, CELAM's Puebla Document partic-ipates in the same trajectory as *Evangelii Nuntiandi*, with its affirmation of the ways in which Vatican II broadened the mention of "seeds of the Word," citing the portion of that apostolic exhorta-tion in which Paul VI addresses the relationship between the Gospel and cultures (*Evangelii Nuntiandi*, No. 20).

In his first encyclical, *Redemptor Hominis*, promulgated in 1979, Pope John Paul II provided further affirmation of the direction marked out by *Ad Gentes*, connecting the positive assess-ment of non-Christian religions expressed in *Nostra Aetate* with the phase Justin coined: "The Fathers of the Church rightly saw in the various religions as it were so many reflections of the one truth, 'seeds of the Word.'"[60] In the spirit of *Ad Gentes*, John Paul II

---

[59] Unlike the lack of attribution about the phrase in *Ad Gentes*, here Paul VI includes a footnote in which he identifies Justin as the source of the expression.

[60] John Paul II, Encyclical Letter *Redemptor Hominis*, March 1979, No. 11, https://www.vatican.va/content/john-paul-ii/en/encyclicals/docu-ments/hf_jp-ii_enc_04031979_redemptor-hominis.html

mentioned "seeds of the Word" three times in *Redemptoris Missio*, his 1990 encyclical "on the permanent validity of the Church's missionary mandate," promulgated to celebrate the twenty-fifth anniversary of the Second Vatican Council's decree on the church's missionary activity. Here too the pope's emphasis was on divine activity in religions other than Christianity. In *Redemptoris Missio* No. 28, he emphasized that the presence and activity of the Holy Spirit are universal, not limited by time or space, reminding us how "The Second Vatican Council recalls that the Spirit is at work in the heart of every person, through the 'seeds of the Word,' to be found in human initiatives—including religious ones—and in [*hu*]mankind's efforts to attain truth, goodness and God himself."[61] Shortly after this, John Paul II describes the broad scope of the Spirit's activity: "The Spirit's presence and activity affect not only the individuals but also society and history, peoples, cultures and religions. Indeed, the Spirit is at the origin of the noble ideals and undertakings which benefit humanity on its journey through history . . . it is the Spirit who sows the 'seeds of the Word' present in various customs and cultures, preparing them for full maturity in Christ." The third mention of the expression in this encyclical also emphasizes the activity of the Spirit as the motive for interreligious dialogue:

> Dialogue does not originate from tactical concerns or self-interest, but is an activity with its own guiding principles, requirements and dignity. It is demanded by deep respect for everything that has been brought about in human beings by the Spirit who blows where he wills. Through

---

[61] John Paul II, Encyclical Letter *Redemptoris Missio*, December 7, 1990, https://www.vatican.va/content/john-paul-ii/en/encyclicals/documents/hf_jp-ii_enc_07121990_redemptoris-missio.html. The encyclical supports this in a footnote that points to *Ad Gentes*, Nos. 3, 11, 15; and *Gaudium et Spes*, Nos. 10–11, 22, 26, 38, 41, 92–93.

dialogue, the Church seeks to uncover the 'seeds of the Word,' a 'ray of that truth which enlightens all [*people*];' these are found in individuals and in the religious traditions of [*hu*]mankind. (*Redemptoris Missio*, No. 56)

The pope's reference to *Nostra Aetate* 2 here, side by side with the invocation of "seeds of the Word" from *Ad Gentes*, emphasizes the need for dialogue that is genuine and not merely tactical or self-interested.[62] In this vein, John Paul II goes on to affirm, "Other religions constitute a positive challenge for the Church: they stimulate her both to discover and acknowledge the signs of Christ's presence and of the working of the Spirit, as well as to examine more deeply her own identity and to bear witness to the fullness of Revelation which she has received for the good of all."[63] This anticipates the appreciation of genuine dialogue as the rich polyhedric *encuentro* proposed by Pope Francis.

This discussion began by asking what relevance a few well-chosen words from a second-century Christian apologist could have for a consideration of twentieth and twenty-first century Latin America. We mapped the path of "seeds of the Word" from the second century through its amplification in the shaping of the

---

[62] In *Redemptoris Missio*, No. 55, John Paul II notes that "dialogue is not in opposition to the mission *ad gentes*; indeed, it has special links with that mission and is one of its expressions."

[63] John Paul II emphasizes that "Those engaged in this dialogue must be consistent with their own religious traditions and convictions, and be open to understanding those of the other party without pretense or close-mindedness, but with truth, humility and frankness, knowing that dialogue can enrich each side. There must be no abandonment of principles nor false irenicism, but instead a witness given and received for mutual advancement on the road of religious inquiry and experience, and at the same time for the elimination of prejudice, intolerance and misunderstandings. Dialogue leads to inner purification and conversion which, if pursued with docility to the Holy Spirit, will be spiritually fruitful" (*Redemptoris Missio*, No. 56).

Second Vatican Council's Decree on the Missionary Activity of the Church. We have also seen how the Second Vatican Council's use of this expression significantly influenced the treatment of indigenous cultures in the documents of CELAM's General Conferences beginning from Medellín in 1968 through Aparecida in 2007. It is this line of thinking that made it from Amazonia to Rome in 2019, finding a place in the Final Document of the Amazonian Synod. The Postsynodal Exhortation *Querida Amazonia* of Pope Francis represents, in some sense, the first—and most authoritative—commentary on the Amazonian Synod, even though, and perhaps unfortunately, the pope deliberately declined to cite the Final Document, instead encouraging people to read it in full.[64] It is to *Querida Amazonia* that we now turn our attention.

Querida Amazonia: Dreaming in the Vernacular

The incarnational orientation of *Querida Amazonia* is unmistakable from the very beginning:

> Everything that the Church has to offer must become incarnate in a distinctive way in each part of the world, so that the Bride of Christ can take on a variety of faces that better manifest the inexhaustible riches of God's grace. Preaching must become incarnate, spirituality must become incarnate, ecclesial structures must become incarnate. (*Querida Amazonia*, No. 6)

---

[64] Pope Francis, Apostolic Exhortation *Querida Amazonia*, February 2, 2020, 2, https://www.vatican.va/content/francesco/en/apost_exhortations/documents/papa-francesco_esortazione-ap_20200202_querida-amazonia.html. Subsequent references to this document will appear parenthetically in the text as *Querida Amazonia*.

This insistence on incarnation, repeated here four times, speaks to the groundedness, the rootedness, the concreteness of each of the four (and interconnected) dreams around which this exhortation is organized: the social dream, the cultural dream, the ecological dream, and the ecclesial dream. Addressing Pope Francis directly in the second person singular, Carmen Nanko-Fernández points out, "Your first sueño is a social dream predicated upon making a preferential option for those who are made poor, marginalized and excluded." Incarnation, in this context, brings an anticolonial imperative according to which "such an option is not one of 'doing for' or 'deciding for' others relegated to the margins of societies," but is instead "a radical affirmation of the agency of those made invisible and deemed incapable of speaking for themselves."[65] Pope Francis insists that the ecological disaster facing Amazonia needs to be addressed holistically and not in isolation from the human dimension, from concerns for the peoples of Amazonia and their well-being. Quoting from *Laudato Si'*, he writes that "a true ecological approach always becomes a social approach; it must integrate questions of justice in debates on the environment, so as to hear both the cry of the earth and the cry of the poor" (*Querida Amazonia*, No. 8, *Laudato Si'*, No. 49).

Once again addressing the pope directly, Nanko-Fernández calls attention to the links he identifies between threats to the environment and threats to the people of the Amazon, which is the path that leads to his consideration of culture and identity:

> You connect the destruction of the environment to the destruction of peoples and cultures, a way of emphasizing that the relationship with creation is a social one,

---

[65] See Carmen Nanko-Fernández, "Querido Francisco: A Theological Response to Your Four Sueños," *National Catholic Reporter*, February 24, 2020, https://www.ncronline.org/opinion/theology-en-la-plaza/querido-francisco

too! This leads to your second dream, a cultural sueño. At a time when too many pundits in the U.S. disparage talk of identity as polarizing, reducing our careful connections between roots and oppressions to shallow charges of identity politics, it is refreshing to see you declare that "identity and dialogue are not enemies."[66]

By sharing his cultural dream in the exhortation, Pope Francis makes what U.S. Latin@ theologians recognize as a preferential option for culture, endorsing and strongly affirming what the Amazonian Synod said, an affirmation that we have traced back through Aparecida and all the way to Medellín.[67] As Nanko-Fernández explains, "Such an option intentionally embraces cultural dimensions of our lives and faiths, a nuanced contextualization that sees en lo popular possibilities of encounter with the divine, expressions of solidarity, epistemologies of struggle."[68] Even without citing the biblical text itself, Pope Francis nods affirmatively in the direction of Romans 1:20 when, in sharing his cultural dream, he writes of how "In each land and its features, God manifests himself and reflects something of his inexhaustible beauty. Each distinct

---

[66] Nanko-Fernández, "Querido Francisco."

[67] On the preferential option for culture in U.S. Latin@ theologies, see María Teresa Dávila, "A 'Preferential Option': A Challenge to Faith in a Culture of Privilege," in *The Word Became Culture*, ed. Miguel H. Díaz (Maryknoll, NY: Orbis Books, 2020), 49–69.

[68] Nanko-Fernández, "Querido Francisco." The preferential option for culture is not emphasized at the expense of the preferential option for poor and marginalized people. Quoting the Puebla Final Document, Pope Francis insists that "Given the situation of poverty and neglect experienced by so many inhabitants of the Amazon region, inculturation will necessarily have a markedly social cast, accompanied by a resolute defence of human rights; in this way it will reveal the face of Christ, who 'wished with special tenderness to be identified with the weak and the poor'" (*Querida Amazonia*, No. 75, quoting *Puebla Document*, No. 196).

group, then, in a vital synthesis with its surroundings, develops its own form of wisdom" (*Querida Amazonia*, No. 32). In the impressive diversity of Amazonian cultures, that wisdom becomes incarnate in so many local vernaculars.

Pope Francis recognizes that Amazonian cultures are at risk from many different directions. He writes, "Just as there are potentialities in nature that could be lost forever, something similar could happen with cultures that have a message yet to be heard, but are now more than ever under threat" (*Querida Amazonia*, No. 28). He insists that cultures do not exist in isolation from each other. In effect, "Our own cultural identity is strengthened and enriched as a result of dialogue with those unlike ourselves. Nor is our authentic identity preserved by an impoverished isolation. Far be it from me to propose a completely enclosed, a-historic, static 'indigenism' that would reject any kind of blending (*mestizaje*)" (*Querida Amazonia*, No. 37). For Francis, the cultures of the peoples of Amazonia are not museum pieces to be carefully curated as though they were dioramas on display. Rather, they are dynamic and open-ended structures of signification that make *buen vivir* possible.

It is when he shares his ecclesial dream that Pope Francis focuses most attentively on Amazonian cultures, emphasizing incarnation as he does from the beginning of *Querida Amazonia*. Here he recognizes that, as the Church grows in Amazonia, it

> constantly reshapes [*its*] identity through listening and dialogue with the people, the realities and the history of the lands in which [*it*] finds [*it*]self. In this way, [*it*] is able to engage increasingly in a necessary process of incul- turation that rejects nothing of the goodness that already exists in Amazonian cultures, but brings it to fulfilment in the light of the Gospel. (*Querida Amazonia*, No. 66)

In a telling footnote, he quotes *Gaudium et Spes* No. 44, in which the Council explains how, very early in its history, the Church learned

> to express the Christian message in the concepts and languages of different peoples . . . this kind of adaptation and preaching of the revealed word must ever be the law of all evangelization. In this way it is possible to create in every country the possibility of expressing the message of Christ in suitable terms and to foster vital contact and exchange between the Church and different cultures.

Pope Francis points out that inculturation—which is, in effect, the incarnation of the Word in specific cultural vernaculars—is not a one-way street. Repeating what he said in *Evangelii Gaudium* No. 115, he insists that "grace supposes culture, and God's gift becomes flesh in the culture of those who receive it" (*Querida Amazonia*, No. 68). The vernacular incarnation that is inculturation involves a "double movement" that includes both the communication of the Gospel "in suitable terms" and a process of reception on the part of the Church whereby the Church is enriched by "the fruits of what the Spirit has already mysteriously sown in that culture" (*Querida Amazonia*, No. 68). This is as close as *Querida Amazonia* comes to explicitly mentioning "seeds of the Word." In that vein, the Church in Amazonia "needs to listen to its ancestral wisdom, listen once more to the voice of its elders, recognize the values present in the way of life of the original communities, and recover the rich stories of its peoples" (*Querida Amazonia*, No. 70).

Francis recognizes that "In the Amazon region, we have inherited great riches from the pre-Columbian cultures," and identifies some of these by quoting from CELAM's Santo Domingo Document: "openness to the action of God, a sense of gratitude for the fruits of the earth, the sacred character of human life and esteem for the family, a sense of solidarity and shared responsibility in common work, the importance of worship, belief in a life beyond this earth, and many other values" (*Querida Amazonia*, No. 70; *Santo Domingo Document*, No. 17). In the Santo Domingo document, these features are identified as "seeds of the Word." To these, Francis himself adds "personal, familial, communal and cosmic harmony and finds expression in a communitarian approach to existence, the ability to find joy and fulfillment in an austere and simple life, and a responsible care of nature that preserves resources for future generations" (*Querida Amazonia*, No. 71).

As for the attitude to be assumed in dreaming into reality "a holiness with Amazonian features, called to challenge the universal Church" (*Querida Amazonia*, No. 77), Pope Francis calls for a "respectful and understanding love" for the peoples of Amazonia and for the practices of popular religion in Amazonia. In that spirit, quoting from *Evangelii Gaudium* No.123, he urges, "Let us not be quick to describe as superstition or paganism certain religious practices that arise spontaneously from the life of peoples. Rather, we ought to know how to distinguish the wheat growing alongside the tares, for 'popular piety can enable us to see how the faith, once received, becomes embodied in a culture and is constantly passed on'" (*Querida Amazonia*, No. 78). This effectively walks back the negative attitude and the disparaging remarks about popular religion that found expression in the 1968 Medellín Final Document.

Francis goes on to say that "It is possible to take up an indigenous symbol in some way, without necessarily considering it as idolatry. A myth charged with spiritual meaning can be used to advantage and not always considered a pagan error" (*Querida Amazonia*, No. 79). It may be hard to conclude for certain that what he had in mind here was to provide a formal response to the charge of idolatry leveled against the Amazonian Synod by its opponents, or to the particular act of cultural violence perpetrated by Alexander Tschugguel in stealing the carvings from Santa Maria in Traspontina and throwing them into the Tiber. Yet there can be no doubt that Pope Francis is calling for a serious rethinking of judgmental attitudes toward symbols and stories "with spiritual meaning" that all too willingly dismiss these as idolatrous or as pagan.[69] Dreaming into reality "a holiness with Amazonian features, called to challenge the universal Church" means that such symbols and such myths, charged with significance in Amazonian vernaculars, should be treated with appropriate respect.

"*Dios te perdone,*" "*plura fecit Deus,*" and "*Verbum caro factum est*" were the three inscriptions that Spanish visitors left behind as evidence of their intercultural *encuentro* on Mona Island in the middle of the sixteenth century. Each of these phrases resonates with new vitality as the Amazon flowed into the Tiber during the Amazonian Synod in October 2019.

---

[69] He adds, though, that "A missionary of souls will try to discover the legitimate needs and concerns that seek an outlet in at times imperfect, partial or mistaken religious expressions, and will attempt to respond to them with an inculturated spirituality." The question that arises from this qualification is a matter of how the "missionary of souls" will diagnose these "legitimate needs and concerns" and what will be involved in the remedy of an "inculturated spirituality."

CONCLUSION

Revelation, a Return to *Amona*

In the introduction to this book, I spoke with respect and gratitude of what I learned from René Latourelle's *Theology of Revelation*. As I consider the itinerary traversed in this much more modest book, I wonder whether my professor would recognize a theology of revelation in these pages. It is from him, after all, that I first learned how important it is to engage in careful retrieval, to map key points in the development of important currents in theology, even if the map I have sketched might seem somewhat unfamiliar to him. As I think of my teacher and mentor Raymond E. Brown, I can imagine how awkward it might be, at least at first, to have had the opportunity to discuss this book with him because he would not be likely to characterize it or recognize it as a work that fits neatly within the disciplinary borders of biblical studies. I also suspect that my dissertation director Ugo Vanni would, with the gentle smile that was the sure sign that there were corrections to be made, tell me how far I had strayed from *Ezekiel in the Apocalypse*, intrigued though he might have been with the apocalyptic currents I mention in these pages.

Brown's lifelong passion for the Johannine literature may have made him curious to know why a Spanish visitor to the island that the Taínos called *Amona* left "*Verbum caro factum est*" as commentary on what he had seen there. For his part, Vanni might have wondered what—if anything—Mona Island has to do with the island of Patmos. No doubt both of these biblical scholars would have been curious about what led me to pay attention to Fray Luis de León. As their student, I would have to admit without the slightest reluctance that the world I inhabit in the twenty-first century is different in many ways from the academic and ecclesiastical milieu of sixteenth-century Spain, but I would vigorously resist the tendency that my twenty-first-century colleagues might have to relegate the work of Fray Luis to the realm of "pre-critical" exegesis in disparaging and dismissing ways.

I would also admit that I found myself fascinated by what I retrieved from the work of Fray Luis, even though that retrieval was limited and selective. His sophisticated passion for language, his stubborn insistence on writing in his own Spanish vernacular, and his commitment to making the Bible accessible to non-elite readers, all at great risk to his own well-being, led me to recognize and appreciate him as a model for the practices of disruptive cartography that this book series advances centuries later. The breadth of his thinking about the Incarnation enriches an appreciation of the extent and the eloquence of God's self-disclosure not only in the Scriptures but throughout all of creation. His articulation of a christology that marveled at the mystery of the Incarnation of the Word leaves me wondering what more Fray Luis might have written if ever he had the opportunity to make his way from Salamanca to the Americas and encounter the vernaculars of its indigenous peoples. Might such an encounter possibly have come to a different appreciation, perhaps even leading him to affirm "Plura fecit Deus" and to recognize the Word at work in the Taíno vernacular in Cave 18?

As it is though, it must be recognized that Fray Luis was no mere bystander in the non-innocent history of the colonization of the Americas. Even though he never left Spain, he was complicit in the shaping of attitudes toward the indigenous peoples of the Americas that continue to bear toxic fruit centuries later, with lasting harm that no apologies can ever hope to undo, even when such apologies come directly from the bishop of Rome. For Fray Luis and most of his Iberian contemporaries, the conversion of the peoples of the "New World" was not an opportunity but an imperative. Fueled by the expectation that it would prepare the way for the return of Christ in glory, the ends were seen to fully justify the means—however harsh and inhumane—just as they had in the *Reconquista* and in the expulsion of those Spanish Jews who refused Christian baptism.

As we have seen, since 1968, the bishops of CELAM have devoted significant effort toward a reconfiguration of the posture of the Church vis-à-vis the indigenous peoples of Latin America, their cultures, their values, their religious practices and expressions. That trajectory become more and more prominent from its beginnings at Medellín, all the way through to Aparecida in 2007, the Fifth General Conference of CELAM at which the then-archbishop of Buenos Aires, Jorge Mario Bergoglio, was a key participant.[1] As we saw by tracing back "seeds of the Word" from Aparecida, to Santo Domingo, to Puebla, and then to Medellín, the Latin American bishops expressed increasingly positive assessments of indigenous cultures. While it would be inaccurate to suggest that "seeds of the Word" is evidence that Justin Martyr was a religious inclusivist, it is equally clear that the expression has acquired considerably greater breadth and depth in the concluding documents of the General Conferences of CELAM as well as in the final document of the Amazonian Synod.

The mention of "culture" became more and more frequent in the concluding documents.[2] Yet the discernment of "seeds of

---

[1] See the important lecture he delivered on January 1, 2008 on "Popular Piety as Inculturation of Faith in the Spirit of Aparecida," in Jorge Mario Bergoglio, *In Your Eyes I See My Words: Homilies and Speeches from Buenos Aires Volume 2: 2005–2008*, ed. Antonio Spadaro, trans. Marina A. Herrera (New York: Fordham University Press, 2020), 233–259.

[2] Bergoglio noted that "In the final document of the Fifth General

the Word" sown in indigenous communities and their cultures has typically focused on evangelization, even with an increasingly supple and well-nuanced understanding of inculturation. The word "revelation" is never explicitly invoked to describe the divine activity that is involved in sowing or nurturing the "seeds of the Word," activity that is ordinarily understood as *praeparatio evangelica* that predisposes peoples and cultures for formal evangelization. While this is also the case in the final document of the Amazon Synod, we find there clear hints of a more intentional reckoning with the action of God in and through the indigenous peoples of Latin America, their cultures, and values, and even their religious practices.[3] Rubén Rosario Rodríguez defines revelation as "a technical term for the concept that knowledge of God originates in a divine act whereby something unknown (or ambiguously apprehended) about God is disclosed, along with the subjective assurance that the content of this revelation is reliable."[4]

The archaeologists who explored Cave 18 on Mona Island were the first to suggest that what they found there represented an early instance of interreligious dialogue during the colonial period. Centuries before *Nostra Aetate*, the Spanish visitors to Cave 18 had

---

Conference the word 'culture' appears around seventy times, and what it seeks to express differs completely from what was understood in the 1950s when the First Conference of the Latin American Bishops was held. Likewise, the reality of popular piety has an impact and a positive resonance that differ greatly from what could be perceived when this same term appeared in the first writings of the Church in Latin America" ("Popular Piety as Inculturation of Faith in the Spirit of Aparecida," 235). The Second Vatican Council was the catalyst for that shift, a shift that gathered momentum all the way from Medellín to Aparecida.

[3] The explicit mention of *teología India*, which was not included in the Aparecida document, is evidence of this.

[4] Rubén Rosario Rodríguez, *Dogmatics after Babel: Beyond the Theologies of Word and Culture* (Louisville, KY: Westminster John Knox, 2018), 131.

no way of knowing that the Second Vatican Council would eventually declare that "The Catholic Church rejects nothing that is true and holy in these religions. She regards with sincere reverence those ways of conduct and of life, those precepts and teachings which, though differing in many aspects from the ones she holds and sets forth, nonetheless often reflect a ray of that Truth which enlightens all" (*Nostra Aetate* 2). Yet, despite the religious intolerance that was the rule in Spain and the dominant practice among their fellow colonizers in the Americas, they chose a different path and adopted a different attitude, one that was also articulated in language that was not unfamiliar in their sixteenth-century cultural, political, and religious milieu.

The Spaniards who left their inscriptions behind in Cave 18 on Mona Island were not theologians lecturing from professorial chairs at Salamanca. Perhaps, though, their intuitions about what God may have been up to in vernacular expressions other than their own—whether or not they could describe it as revelation—may have something to offer that reaches across the centuries. It was precisely their Christian frame of reference, which they articulated in terms that were not unfamiliar in their own sixteenth-century Spanish milieu, that opened them to see not idolatry that had to be contested or erased in the name of Christ and the Gospel, but clues to the possibility that the works of God might be even greater than they could have imagined or understood.

Index

Jean-Pierre Ruiz teaches on the faculty of the Department of Theology and Religious Studies at St. John's University in New York, where he is also a senior research fellow of the Vincentian Center for Church and Society. He is a noted Nuyorican biblical scholar and theologian, and his publications include the Catholic Press Association Award–winning book *Readings from the Edges: The Bible and People on the Move*. A past president of the Academy of Catholic Hispanic Theologians of the U.S. (ACHTUS), he received their Virgilio Elizondo Award for distinguished achievement in theology. During the Obama administration, Ruiz served as a member of the U.S. Department of State's Working Group on Religion and Foreign Policy. Ruiz's research interests include the Apocalypse of John, the place of the Bible in the colonization of the Americas, the Bible and migration, and interreligious dialogue (especially Jewish–Christian dialogue).